THE MACHINE

HOW TO BUILD AND SCALE ANY ESTABLISHED SERVICE BUSINESS

STEVE HACKNEY

Foreword by
Richard Brewin

i

THE MACHINE
HOW TO BUILD AND SCALE ANY ESTABLISHED SERVICE BUSINESS

ISBN 978-0-9567907-7-4

Published in the UK by TCA Business Books

TCA
PUBLISHING

DEDICATION

To Mum and Dad. Thank you so much for everything.

To Pete, Rob, Julia and our entire team ... I couldn't have done this without you. You'll never know how much I appreciate and love you all.

To my wife, Helen, who has been a rock throughout my career. I love you so much.

To my amazing children, Thomas, Matthew and Liv ... you drive me each day to be the best version of myself!

To the hundreds of business coaches, consultants and mentors we help and support around the world ... you ensure we never get complacent, and keep pushing the bar higher and higher.

And last but not least, to our clients. This book is really dedicated to all of you. Without you, there would be no MACHINE. Without you, I would never have been able to create the breakthrough system thousands of owners of service businesses use to change their lives and those around them. I can't thank you enough.

TABLE OF CONTENTS

INTRODUCTION...x

CHAPTER 1: WHY SERVICE BUSINESSES STOP
            GROWING...21

CHAPTER 2: INTRODUCTION TO THE MACHINE............29

CHAPTER 3: THE PERFECT CLIENT AVATAR.................43

CHAPTER 4: SELLING THE INVISIBLE: PRODUCTISING
            YOUR SERVICES..83

CHAPTER 5: THE GROWTH CONTINUUM.........................95

CHAPTER 6: LEAD GENERATION SYSTEM......................99

CHAPTER 7: CONVERSION SYSTEM 205

CHAPTER 8: MAXIMISING CLIENT VALUE....................237

CHAPTER 9: PUTTING YOUR GROWTH ON
            AUTOPILOT 273

CHAPTER 10: THE SCALING UP PARAMETERS...............291

CHAPTER 11: PUMP THE MACHINE WITH
            CHANNELS AND TACTICS...........................293

CHAPTER 12: APPLYING THE SCIENCE OF
            MARGINAL GAINS...311

CHAPTER 13: SYSTEMS, SYSTEMS, SYSTEMS 339

CHAPTER 14: STAFFING THE EXPANSION..................... 351

CHAPTER 15: THE PERFECT SCALING UP MODEL 371

CHAPTER 16: PUTTING IT ALL TOGETHER..................... 381

CHAPTER 17: THE NEXT LEVEL AND BEYOND.............. 385

OTHER RESOURCES.. 391

FOREWORD

By Richard Brewin

2021 saw me enter my fifth decade in the accountancy profession, the first 28 years at the sharp end in professional practice and, since then, as a mentor and coach to accountants across the globe. I'm one of that minority of people who love having conversations with accountants about themselves!

Accountants, like all service providers, face the challenge of 'selling' things that are difficult to see – expertise, support, reassurance. Steve refers to it in this book as 'selling the invisible', and it means that to be successful, service businesses have to do things differently to conventional product-based enterprises. We can't just follow 'normal' business and growth rules.

In my experience, there comes a point in the life of every accounting firm and any service business where growth stalls or flatlines. Despite all the best endeavours of those at the top, the things that have seen them grow successfully in the past fail to get them over the next climb.

I see this happen all the time. It's common to every service business. I see it now, and I saw it all those years ago when we worked with hundreds of businesses when running our own accounting firms.

Steve calls this phenomenon the 'Service Business Growth Curve', and if you're going to take your service business to where you envisaged when you started, it's the reason why you have to do things differently.

And it really matters, especially today. 2020 was a year like no other. It's changed us all and, for many, changed our priorities. Having a business that reflects your vision and your goals has never been so important. The compromise that many accountants and owners of other service firms have learned to live with, the inability to reach our goals, doesn't hack it any longer. We want to be happy. We want to improve the lives of those around us.

I work with my accounting clients and members to make sure they break through this 'brick wall' of frustration that stands in the way of true satisfaction for them. One thing that they will already be doing well within their firms will be their compliance, their production processes, if you like. They do this well because they systemise the process. To help them move through the barriers to growth and fulfil their dreams, they need to take a lesson from this and implement a system for growth.

The challenge, of course, is that it's not that easy putting a system in place that works 24/7, especially when almost every service business owner or owners have little expertise in this area, have little time to spare and lack the confidence to dive into such an approach.

As you'll soon see from this book, Steve has the solution. He has refined THE MACHINE over decades, and when you apply it to your own service business, you'll put your business back on the right path and never look back.

There are a number of people who promise results. Steve doesn't just promise; he delivers. The success of our own accounting firms is testament to that. THE MACHINE works, and you just need to provide the fuel!

Richard Brewin, FCA
Progress BB
www.progressbb.co.uk

INTRODUCTION

Selling the invisible. That's what we do. When you break it down, there's nothing more challenging than selling hot air. But you and I do it, day-in, day-out. We sell intangible services.

Unlike any product ...

they can't be seen,

they can't be touched, and

they can't be smelt.

Make no mistake, there's nothing harder to sell than a service.

My first job, after graduating from Loughborough University in 1990, was selling photo copiers for Canon. At 21 years old I was a very green salesman, but Canon back then had a phenomenal sales training division. It was headed by a chap called Ernie Bones, and to this day he is one of the best sales trainers I've ever had the pleasure of working with.

But, on reflection, he had an easy job ...

Canon manufactured the finest and most efficient photocopiers on the planet. Xerox and Panasonic came close, but the reality was that Canon stood head and shoulders above every other manufacturer.

The seven-day training course was split into four days of 'product' training and three days of 'sales' training.

The product training was simply structured so we could learn everything we had to know about the Canon range of photocopiers. There were live product demonstrations. Top engineers would come and show us the inner workings of THE MACHINEs. Every make and model was on show in the training showroom so we could all 'have a play'. Ernie would list all the features and corresponding benefits of each copier, and we simply had to learn them.

In its simplest form, all you had to do was place your piece of paper face down on the glass and press a button, and THE MACHINE would take care of the rest. Then, out popped a high-quality identical copy or copies.

Then the sales training kicked in.

Most of the time, Ernie took us through how to cold call, which back then, consisted of either picking up the phone or pounding the streets to find prospects. And when we did find someone who was interested, the first step – and always the first step – was to arrange a demonstration.

Ernie constantly reinforced that the purpose of cold calling was not to sell a copier but to book a demonstration. That was 75% of the sale there and then.

Why?

Because Canon's photocopiers not only worked better than the competition but also looked stunning. You got one of those babies into an office, and people just visualised having it as part of the office furniture. Ernie repeated, 'get a demonstration, and closing the deal is almost assured'.

Of course, when we were 'in the field', it wasn't as easy as that, especially the cold calling (which I hated, by the way), but sure enough, when you got a demonstration, the closing rates were exceptionally high.

I remember those days fondly. Back then, I was an elite rugby player. I played for Leicester Tigers, one of the most successful rugby union teams in Europe. But rugby was amateur in those days, so we, of course, had to work to put food on the table!

My 'right hand man' was Martin Johnson. 'Johnno' would go on to lead England to World Cup glory in 2003, but in 1991 he would be seen with me, lugging photocopiers around the streets of Leicester and Nottingham (fairly large cities in the UK).

You seriously can't imagine some of the challenges we faced trying to carry huge machines up flights of stairs. It reminds me of that funny scene in the US sitcom, *Friends* when Ross, along with the gang, is trying to get a new settee up a flight of stairs to his apartment on the top floor. He's shouting 'pivot, pivot' pivot' as they try to turn round each corner of the staircase. Ultimately, they fail, they drop the settee because it's so big and heavy, and it breaks in two. Believe me, there were more than just a handful of those incidents when we were struggling to get the larger machines into office blocks with no lifts!

Anyway, the point I'm making is the demonstration was nine-tenths of the sale. Because a copier is a tangible product and because Canon's machines were the best on the market at the time, just giving a live demo of them (even when sweat is dripping off your nose!) was by far the best way to sell it.

And I'd discover soon after that selling products was so much easier than selling services.

You see, having carved out a successful few years selling photocopiers, I then moved to selling commercial insurance.

It was like night and day.

Even though I had access to the world's leading insurance companies and their insurance policies, you couldn't do a live demo of them!

I'd moved from selling the visible to selling the invisible, and that required a new set of skills, none of which I had learned when selling for Canon.

But because I was working for one of the UK's most successful commercial insurance brokers (now part of Gallagher's, who currently have an annual revenue of over $7 billion), the top insurance companies would send their top sales trainers to teach us how to sell their policies.

And what did they do? They did everything they could to transform EVERY insurance POLICY into an insurance 'PRODUCT'.

Because they knew if they could make it more tangible, it was simply easier to sell.

... and, of course, it was.

It was a learning experience I'd never forget, and it would serve me well once rugby union finally turned professional in 1995.

That's when I decided to set up my first business ... Hackney Marketing. I was 27 at the time and knew I'd probably have only three or four years as a professional rugby player, so it made sense for me to set up a business that I could grow slowly, so that once my rugby career ended, I could seamlessly transition into a business owner.

In my first book, *The FORMULA*, I detail the process of how I did that. But one of the best decisions I ever made was that I would focus all my attention on helping service businesses to grow.

That seemed logical to me.

I'd been taught some of the best techniques and strategies that the biggest insurance companies could offer and that few others had access to, and I identified a gap in the market.

I learned that very few people specialised in helping service businesses to grow.

And that led to my first 'product'.

I was, of course, selling consulting services, but I transformed that expertise into a course or a PRODUCT. I called it the POWER Marketing System: The Proven and Guaranteed Process to Grow Your Service Business (see Figures 1 and 2).

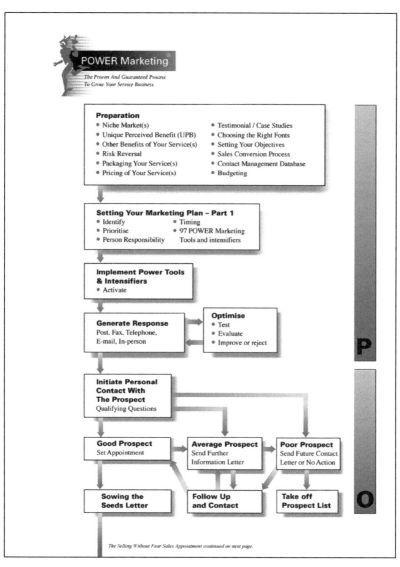

Figure 1. The POWER Marketing System for Service Businesses

Figure 2. The Audio Programme

That course put me on the map, so to speak, and even though the internet was still brand new (CERN only having given us the World Wide Web in 1993), I was still able to sell it throughout 46 different countries.

And ever since then, I've been honing, learning, developing and perfecting growth, and scaling expertise for any service business.

That expertise is now a system called THE MACHINE, and together with my long-term business partner Peter Finlay, it's helped us build and sell Europe's largest franchise consulting group, build the world's largest marketing network of accountants, build one of the world's largest and most successful agencies for coaches and mentors (with more than 1500 worldwide) and helped countless thousands of service business owners take their firms to the next level.

But whereas my first book, *The FORMULA*, helped NEW businesses, THIS book is focused on the more challenging aspect of growing an *established* service business.

You see, as you know only too well, starting a service business is relatively easy.

Of course, it comes with its challenges, but the real challenges start when you want to take it to the next level and beyond.

You've reached that point already.

For reasons that will soon become apparent, your growth has stifled or isn't accelerating as fast as you'd like. You've probably tried a number of things without success, and you've (luckily) come across this book.

In fact, this book is for you if you're currently suffering from any one or more of these challenges ...

- You've reached a point in the growth of your business where no matter what you try, you can't seem to create any lasting further development.
- Your business isn't giving you the income and lifestyle you desire.
- Your business isn't giving you the financial and personal freedom to choose how to live your life.
- You're working all hours, and it doesn't seem to make a difference.
- You lie in bed at night worrying about your cash flow and paying outstanding invoices.

- Referrals have dried up, or they're not as frequent as they used to be.
- You're looking to exit the business, but you need to maximise its value before sale.
- You have no repeatable and systemised method of generating leads or clients.
- You're losing more clients than you're currently acquiring.
- You've fallen out of love with your business.
- Acquiring new clients is harder than ever.
- When you do acquire new clients, you always seem to be squeezed on fees.
- And so on!

The good news is that in this book there's a solution for every one of these challenges (and more).

Growth alone is not the complete solution, although more sales, and especially profit, will solve most of the above. There are, however, other factors to consider too, and we'll also be covering those.

One thing I can promise you is this ...

When you begin installing THE MACHINE into your established service business, you will see an instant transformation in it, and as you apply more and more of the elements contained in THE MACHINE, your business will grow and develop beyond your wildest expectations ... but, of course, you have to implement it.

You see, reading this book ... underlining sentences or paragraphs ... turning the corner of important pages, and so on ... won't do anything for you and your business. Action is all that matters.

And although THE MACHINE is a proven blueprint for taking your service business to the next level and beyond ... without action from YOU, nothing changes. However, I have a surprise for you at the end of the book which just may suit you!

Anyway, let's get started ...

CHAPTER 1

WHY SERVICE BUSINESSES STOP GROWING

When we created the world's largest marketing network for accountants, it involved one of the largest research projects we'd ever undertaken, which was to understand the evolution of a typical firm. We found that although most accounting firms would often enjoy good, even rapid growth in the early years, they'd more often than not eventually hit a brick wall, and growth would slow or even stop altogether.

We discovered a pattern of development and growth that almost every firm experienced, and I'm not exaggerating. The research was so revealing and, to be honest, very exciting to us.

It meant that we could predict the growth curve of every accounting firm in the world and, therefore, we could influence their growth as soon as we understood where they were on the curve.

We then extended the research to hundreds of business sectors to see if we could apply the model to other industries. And we were astonished to find that whereas product-based businesses were unaffected, the same pattern occurred with ANY service-based business.

Now, in case you're wondering if this was one of those 'eight out of ten' type basic research projects where we asked 100 people, let me say that when you have an army of accounting firms (just over 1500 of them), each with, on average, 250 business clients, the market size for the research project was huge. Of course, we didn't analyse every business, but we did analyse thousands of them with qualitative and quantitative research, questionnaires, and so on. It literally mirrored what we found to be happening in accounting firms, and, as you're about to see, your service business will mirror what I call the 'Service Business Growth Curve'.

The model shows how a typical service business evolves and why the frustration starts to mount as growth slows.

I think you'll find this fascinating, too ...

So, exactly why do service businesses stop growing? What's the root cause?

Well, I'm afraid to say ... **it's YOU**!

Let me explain ...

I'm guessing the reason you started your business in the first place is because you've developed an area of expertise which improves the lives or businesses of others and you wanted to share and monetise it.

Why Service Businesses STOP Growing

You love delivering your services and seeing the positive effect they have on your clients ... right?

And in those early years, you had the time and energy to generate leads and acquire your clients ... and you probably enjoyed doing it, right?

Once you got your clients, they had your full attention as you made sure your services were delivered to them as best as they possibly could be.

Word spread about you and as result, clients were relatively easy to acquire and referrals were plentiful because you were working closely with your clients and delivering an outstanding level of service. You were on the crest of a wave.

But as your business grew, and you increased the size of your team, you're squeezing the one commodity that you can't expand, your time. You're being pulled from pillar to post. You're doing most, if not all, of the client acquisition. You're trying to service clients. You're trying to manage a team of people, suppliers and finance. You're still trying to generate leads, you may have outside help or even team members to do it, but it's just not as effective as it once was because you haven't the time to devote to it and give it your full attention. You've probably thought about the good old days and how much easier and more enjoyable it was back then. It's now exhausting and unfortunately... you, your team, your clients and your business are all suffering as a result.

THE MACHINE

Whether you have business partners or not... **the business is all about <u>YOU</u>** therefore there's no capacity to grow because you simply don't have the luxury of time or any capacity to do more.

Whether you like or not... you're now running a personality-based business that has ultimately reached a point where you can't do any more. This is what the personality bubble is. It looks slightly different for every person, but the problems are the same. You and your business have **hit a brick wall** and unless you <u>change</u>, there's no way for you to take the business to the next level.

Now you may have reached this point already, or you're heading towards it. Either way don't worry there is a solution and it's easier than you may think to apply.

To explain further, take a look at the illustration shown in Figure 1.1. This is the Service Business Growth Curve ... and **<u>EVERY</u>** service business is somewhere on it.

In all probability, right now you're somewhere between points 'A' and 'B', or you've flatlined at 'C', or worse still you're shrinking ... you're somewhere between 'B' and 'D'.

The personality bubble is every point between A and D and it's why you can't break free and start the journey to point E.

Incidentally, if you're currently somewhere between the start and point 'A', enjoy it! But be mindful that prior to reaching point 'A' you must burst the bubble and apply what I'm about to reveal to you in this book.

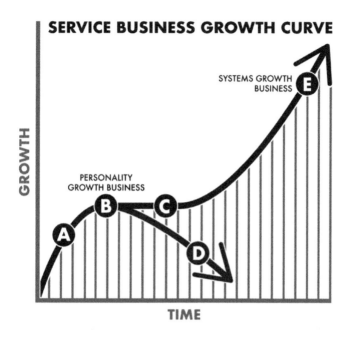

Figure 1.1. The Service Business Growth Curve

And all of our clients, experienced the same frustrations you're having, but **when you realise where you are on the Growth Curve**, you can take steps to get back on track and head towards point 'E' and beyond.

Many of our clients were in the bubble too.

They just didn't know it or what to do to break free. Some tried and no doubt like you, they tried hard.

They appointed marketing managers or directors or worked with agencies or business coaches, but nothing really worked and they were thinking... "It's as though I have no control over my growth whatsoever, regardless of how many hours I work or who I listen to. They all talk a good game, but no-one delivers!"

The thing is, as I've just explained, whilst your business is in the personality bubble, very little you do to try to move the business forward actually has a lasting impact because you don't have the capacity.

The only way to free you from the bubble is to transition from a *personality growth business* into a **systems growth business**.

And to do that you need THE MACHINE!

So, let's first take a high-level view of THE MACHINE so you can get a good understanding of what you'll be implementing over the coming weeks and months to ensure you get your service business back on track and moving quickly to point E on the Service Business Growth Curve …

Chapter Summary and Action Points

- Re-read this chapter to fully understand why your service business has stopped growing.

- Your service business is right now at some point along the Service Business Growth Curve.

- Take responsibility for the position your business is in. You cannot and must not blame anything outside your control (pandemics, economy, low staff numbers, and so on). You are and must be the only person who can drive your firm forward.

- You're not reaching your growth and income targets because you're a *personality growth business trapped in the 'Personality Bubble'*. You need to make the transition to a *systems growth business.*

- Understand that as long as you have the right attitude (this WILL work for me, rather than this will never work in my service business), then, no matter where your business is on the Growth Curve, you can take steps to overcome any challenge you have by implementing the advice in this book.

- Your goal now is to transform your business into a *systems growth* organisation and put it on a path towards point E on the Service Business Growth Curve. You'll do that by implementing THE MACHINE!

THE MACHINE

CHAPTER 2

INTRODUCTION TO THE MACHINE

As I mentioned in the introduction, my very first system for building service businesses was called POWER Marketing. Back in the late nineties and early noughties, it was a phenomenally successful approach for growing any service business. But, of course, back then the internet was only just gathering pace, and much of what we all needed to do to acquire clients and scale our businesses was focused primarily offline rather than online.

However, because I was using the internet, as well as traditional tactics such as direct mail and print advertising (see typical example ad in Figure 2.1), I was starting to build my experience of online methods.

Back then, the internet was like the Wild West!

I was one of the first to use pay per click (PPC) advertising. One of the first pioneers of PPC was a company called Overture (which was subsequently acquired by Yahoo!).

Free Report For Accountants Reveals The Secrets Of...

"How To Quickly And Easily Get A Constant Stream Of New Clients And More Fee Income From Existing Clients - Guaranteed"

Let's face it, there are just two things which determine your success - getting profitable new clients and generating as much income as you can from your existing clients.

How good you are as an accountant is unfortunately not as important. Why would I say this?

Being A Brilliant Accountant Counts For Very Little

Here's the stark reality - even the best Accountant in the world will go broke without a constant stream of new clients and more fee income from existing clients. It's that simple.

The sad **truth** is most people rarely achieve just one of these things, never mind both of them.

The "Secret" Ingredient

It's a familiar story, yet the **key** to your success is NOT to improve your expertise or even the service levels of your staff. No. The key is for you to become a sales and marketing whiz. That's right you heard me right - And yes - you can do it! Here's the **proof**...

"Thanks to your 'secret' sales and marketing approach, we have acquired 76 new clients and are averaging 6 new clients per month. This will generate approx £418,000 fee income over the next 5 years. Our average fee income has jumped from £850 to over £1,100."
Rowena Barnwell, Partner
Barnwell Brewin, Ashby

Becoming a sales and marketing expert is a reality I'm sure you're very **uncomfortable** with. In fact I can already hear you saying things like, "I can't do that. I can't do all this stuff and learn about marketing. I just can't see myself ever becoming a marketing genius."

Unfortunately that's what most people say. And that's why most people **fail** or never reach their personal and business goals.

Heck most accountants don't even like sales and marketing. They think

"sell" is a four letter word they'd rather not deal with, and "marketing" is always someone elses job!

Even those that are good at selling don't ever reach their potential because they simply don't have enough prospects to visit. **Why?** Because their marketing isn't churning out a steady supply of prospects who are "desperate" to find the right accountant.

What's The Answer?

What if I said there was a sales and marketing system that once in place runs on **auto-pilot**, and automatically contains the essential and proven business building techniques needed to guarantee your success? Would you be interested?

What if I said this system contained 103 (yes - one - hundred - and - three) different strategies built into it? Every one a critical and important part of what I call the "**success jigsaw**."

Having Sales And Marketing Experience Is Irrelevant

What if I said you needed **no** sales and marketing expertise to create this unbeatable sales and marketing system? You'd be sceptical no doubt, but I'm sure you'd be intrigued.

What if I said this approach has been **100%** successful for every accountant and every other service business provider who has used the system? And the results could be backed up and fully verified. Would you be interested?

How To Guarantee Your Success

I bet you would - even though you may have your reservations. But surely this system doesn't exist does it? **Yes it does!** However, you're probably already doubting much of what I've said. And why wouldn't you?

From time to time we all hear of some hyped up business growth strategy, that turns out to be no better than our worst fears. But I'm not asking you to believe how successful this system is now. All the

details are inside my **FREE Report**.

FREE Report Shows You How...

My **FREE report** titled, *"High Profit Secrets: How To Get A Constant Stream Of New Clients And More Fee Income From Existing Clients"* will help. Inside this exciting report you'll discover...

1. The **vital ingredients** that guarantee your success, and how to use each one in a simple and powerful growth system

2. How to use the three "**Success Keys**" to skyrocket your sales and profits

3. The four "**Income Stream Generators**," and using them to catapult your practice forward

4. How many of the best and mostly secret practice growth strategies are actually FREE to use. I've identified 67 of them for you!

5. How a simple 6 stage "**Selling Without Fear Sales Appointment**" can transform your client acquisitions

6. And **dozens** more secrets revealed

Get Your FREE Copy Right Now

TO GET YOUR FREE COPY of this exciting report, call my **free recorded message** (24 hours) on **0808 1449797**. Alternatively ~~complete this~~ coupon and post it back to me at the address below.

☐ *Yes!* Please send me your FREE Special Report. I want to discover the proven practice growth secrets I can use

First Name: (Mr/Mrs/Ms)

Surname:

Company:

Address:

Tel:

Send To: Hackney Marketing Ltd,
FREEPOST MID 18761, LEICESTER.
LE3 2ZJ. Tel: 0116 239 4433   GP 1

Figure 2.1. POWER Marketing Print Ad

Back then, you could buy traffic for 1 cent per visitor (I kid you not!). But the PPC model was unsophisticated, prone to abuse (people were known to employ a team of people to simply click on their competitors' ads to significantly increase their ad spend!) and didn't deliver targeted visitors like it does now.

Of course, Google (formed in 1998) changed the landscape forever, and today, social media platforms, video, online advertising, and so on now dominate the online marketing and advertising landscape, which is great news for marketers like me, because prior to then we had to rely on traditional methods to acquire clients.

Today, there are, of course, both online and offline routes to market, but back in the days of my POWER Marketing System, tactics and strategies were all non-internet based.

So, by 2003, my system was outdated!

Fortunately, as I said, I began using the internet way back in 1997, so I was building up a level of expertise that few others had.

And in 2004 through a mutual client, I met Peter, who was aware of my work with service businesses and wanted my advice on a business he was looking to launch. Pete was and still is one of the world's leading authorities on franchising and licensing (he licensed Coke in the UK and franchised the likes of BT and other well-known brands).

His business idea was to create a new way to build a franchise consultancy, and following a few weeks of negotiation, together with Howard Flint, Peter's existing business partner, a former army officer and brilliant operations expert, we jointly set up *The Franchise Group*.

Central to my involvement was for me to run the marketing side of the business using the POWER Marketing System.

By the end of 2004, the system was firing on all cylinders, using both online and offline tactics and strategies (back then there were still no social media platforms. Facebook, for example, would not be launched to the general public until 2006).

Google had launched its first iteration of Google AdWords (now known as Google Ads) in 2000, and it quickly became a major force in online marketing. It was still relatively unsophisticated, but it would deliver huge volumes of relatively targeted traffic.

We used a number of both online and offline tactics to grow the business. In terms of acquiring franchise consultants (franchisees) Google Ads would prove to be our primary source. Even back in 2005/6/7, we were spending around £30,000 a month, but it was delivering us a huge return on investment (known as ROAS).

We spent just over £900,000 on Google Ads over a period of 30 months, but it generated 90 franchisees, each paying either £60,000 or £45,000. Not too shabby!

We also used Google Ads to generate clients (business owners looking to franchise their businesses). We also used a number of offline tactics such as direct mail, print advertising (see example ad in Figure 2.2) and fax advertising (yep FAX! See an example fax in Figure 2.3). We were sending around 200,000 faxes per week back then (it's such a shame that fax marketing is redundant now, and, as you can see, handwritten faxes worked brilliantly).

By the way, there are so many lessons to be learned from these examples in terms of what you need to do to grow and scale your service business, and I will, of course, be covering them with you in greater detail throughout this book.

By mid-2007, we were working with more than 125 clients, helping them to franchise their businesses.

Almost all were service-based businesses, and each one successfully implemented the POWER Marketing System (now utilising more and more online tactics and strategies) to grow their own businesses, acquire franchisees and help the franchisees grow their businesses.

We sold The Franchise Group in September 2007, and after taking a few months out, Pete and I decided to use the POWER Marketing System to help as many people as we could.

That's when we decided to create a network of accountants who, in turn, would give all their business clients access to The Vault (our online training version of the POWER Marketing System).

But this was just the start. I knew the POWER Marketing System could be improved significantly. It was relatively complicated back then and needed to be simplified.

Figure 2.2. Franchisee Print Ad

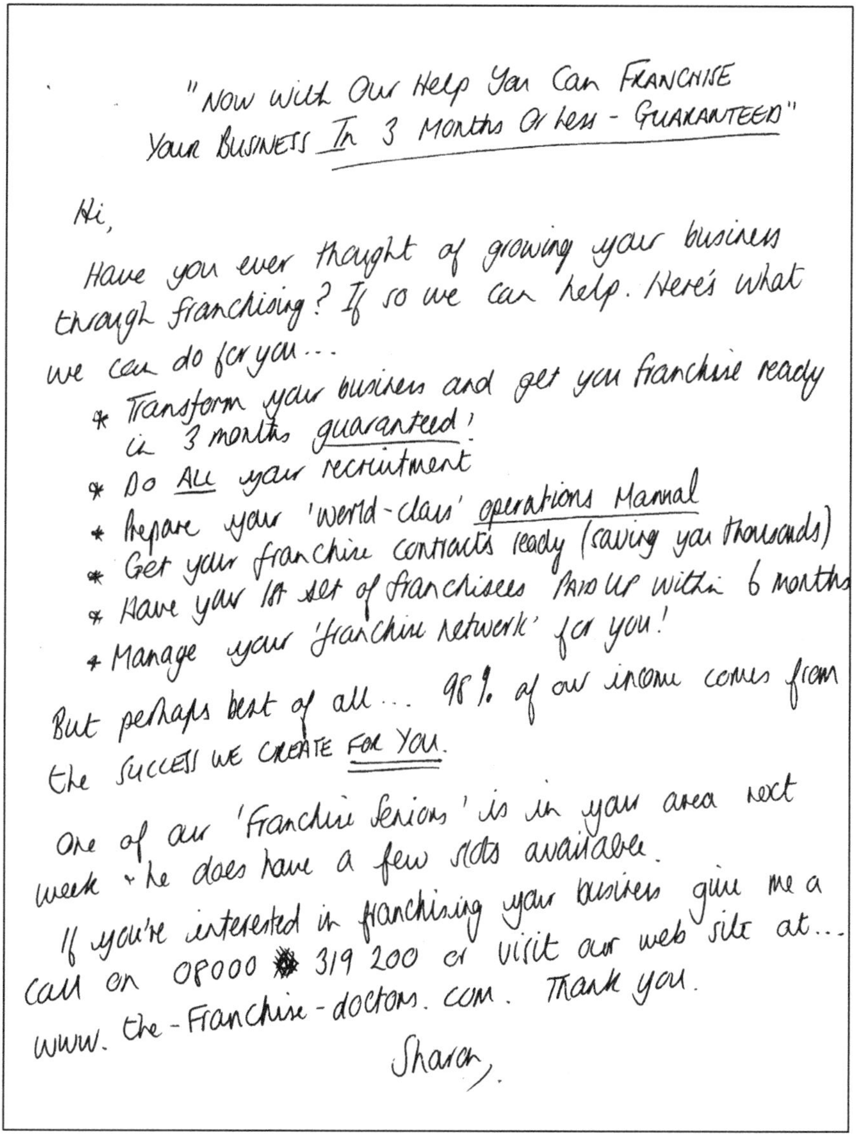

"Now with Our Help You Can FRANCHISE Your BUSINESS In 3 Months Or Less - GUARANTEED"

Hi,

Have you ever thought of growing your business through franchising? If so we can help. Here's what we can do for you...

* Transform your business and get you franchise ready in 3 months guaranteed!
* Do ALL your recruitment
* Prepare your 'world-class' operations Manual
* Get your franchise contracts ready (saving you thousands)
* Have your 1st set of franchisees paid up within 6 months
* Manage your 'franchise network' for you!

But perhaps best of all... 98% of our income comes from the SUCCESS WE CREATE FOR YOU.

One of our 'Franchise Seminars' is in your area next week + he does have a few slots available.

If you're interested in franchising your business give me a call on 08000 ✹ 319 200 or visit our web site at... www.the-Franchise-doctors.com. Thank you.

Sharon,

Figure 2.3. Franchise Lead Generation Fax

Some tactics and strategies didn't work for every kind of business (product-based businesses were using it during this time as well).

And that's when we decided to conduct one of the largest tests ever carried out for any marketing system. Because we were working with just under 1500 accountants around the world, each with, on average, 250 business clients, we had a market sample size close to 375,000 businesses. Of course, not all businesses used the system, but around 45% did.

Clients would report results back to their accountants during review meetings, who, in turn, reported the data to us.

And over a period of around 18 months we compiled a total picture of what worked, what didn't and a whole load of other things.

This led to the simplification of the system, and over a period of several years The FORMULA was born (I go into great detail about The FORMULA in my book with the same title).

The FORMULA is still in existence today (see Figure 2.4) and is a phenomenally successful business growth system for start-up and young businesses (basically ensuring they get on the Growth Curve up to point A and on their way to point B).

I have trained more than 1500 coaches, consultants and mentors on The FORMULA (and continue to do so today) and they are influencing and helping in the main service businesses all over the world to implement The FORMULA into their businesses.

The FORMULA

(T × L × C × M) S

=

EXPONENTIAL GROWTH

T – Transform Existing Strategies
L – Lead Generation
C – Conversion
M – Maximise Client Value
S – Systemise and Automate

Figure 2.4. The FORMULA

And although The FORMULA will ensure any business owner that applies it will get exponential growth once they're established and reaching point A on the Growth Curve, the problems I alluded to earlier in Chapter 1 start to raise their heads.

So, I needed to develop a system that would eradicate most of those challenges, one that could take any established service business to the next level and beyond. And this is where my 'Done-For-You Client Programme' came to the fore.

For the last decade I've been working on a one-to-one basis (with the support of my growing in-house team of experts) with my clients. During this time, I've focused on the most efficient and successful way to grow and scale any established service business, so they avoid the pitfalls outlined in the Growth Curve.

And it's during this time that THE MACHINE was born.

It obviously includes the components of The FORMULA (why reinvent the wheel when it works so well?); however, other elements have been added to create a system which overcomes every growth and scaling challenge that all established service business suffer from and then automatically accelerates the development of the business with minimal input from the business owners.

Figure 2.5 shows the high-level view of THE MACHINE …

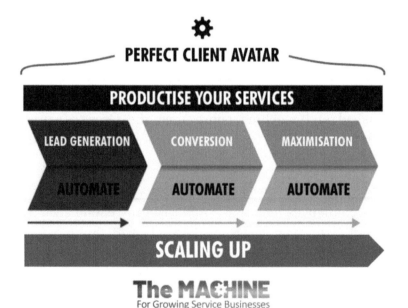

Figure 2.5. THE MACHINE

Let me quickly take you through it, and then, in the following chapters, we'll break down each component of THE MACHINE so you're able to implement each part into your own service business ...

Perfect Client Avatar

The fuel for THE MACHINE is what I call your Perfect Client Avatar. In short, you identify the Perfect Clients you're looking to acquire and then build THE MACHINE around them.

This ensures you make it so much easier to acquire the *right* clients at the *right* fee and enables you to capture a big slice of that market.

Productise Your Services

One of the most effective strategies to help you differentiate your service business from all others and make your services easier to buy is to transform your intangible services into tangible 'products'.

Lead Generation System

Once you've identified your Perfect Client Avatar and Productised Your Services, you're in position to target those Perfect Clients and deliver a laser-focused message to them. You'll use your expertise to grab their attention, followed by a step-by-step 'Lead Generation System', to convert them from prospects into high-quality leads.

Conversion System

As soon as a lead is acquired, your 'Conversion System' kicks in. You'll put in place a series of strategic steps, beautifully choreographed to ensure a high percentage of leads convert into clients at the right fee.

Maximising Client Value System

Once the client is acquired, your 'Maximising Client Value System' takes over. Again, you'll use a series of proven steps to secure the client, delight and wow them, retain them for longer and then ethically sell more of your services to them.

Automate

Once your three systems are in place, you'll then use leading-edge software and applications to automate all the non-human elements.

This ensures THE MACHINE runs on autopilot. Figuratively speaking, once you automate THE MACHINE you then turn the key, and it runs and runs, even while you sleep or you're on holiday. Automation is key to priming THE MACHINE ready for scaling.

Scaling Up

Now, with THE MACHINE fully systemised and automated, you're ready to scale. Think of this as transforming THE MACHINE from small to large (see Figure 2.6) but without the normal growing pains.

You're simply applying several scaling-up tactics (I call them 'Scaling-Up Parameters'), and because all the efficiencies are already built into THE MACHINE, your business will increase in size in line with your own objectives and goals for your business.

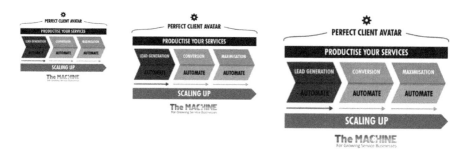

Figure 2.6. Using THE MACHINE to Grow

And that's the overview of THE MACHINE.

I hope that's got you all excited for what really is possible when you implement THE MACHINE into your own service business.

The rest of the book will break down each part of THE MACHINE to enable you to implement it piece by piece, step by step ...

Chapter Summary and Action Points

- Re-read this chapter to get a good understanding of the component parts of THE MACHINE.

- THE MACHINE is so successful because it's a complete approach for growing your established service business. It addresses and overcomes every problem identified by the Growth Curve, and it puts you on the right path.

- Your growth is fully systemised and automated, making it easier for you to scale once you're ready.

THE MACHINE

CHAPTER 3

THE PERFECT CLIENT AVATAR

When I transitioned from being a photocopier salesman to commercial insurance broker, I remember being invited to a two-day training event in London organised by Zurich, one of the big players in the commercial insurance market at the time. The title of the training was simply, 'Bespoke Insurance Products'.

Prior to the training, I had no idea what it would focus on, but I was intrigued by what they meant by the words 'bespoke' and 'products'.

The first session was really interesting, and I still remember it as if it were only yesterday.

It was called 'Market Penetration and Dominance', and the trainers took us through the most effective method they had to quickly penetrate specific markets and then dominate them.

It was fascinating (and remember back then my 'day job' was playing elite rugby!).

THE MACHINE

What really stuck in my mind was how Zurich would focus on one particular sector of the market, such as builders or haulage companies, and develop an insurance policy (they called them 'products', which we'll discuss in detail in the next chapter) to fit that market like a glove.

They would then develop a marketing strategy for the insurance brokers to use to roll out the 'product' to the specific market.

It sounds so obvious now, but I can tell you, this is something so few service businesses do (actually every type of business).

I remember getting back from the training eager for us to launch both the haulage and builder products. I agreed with my sales director (Les Cusworth, former Leicester Tigers and England legend and still good friend) that we would first target builders and then haulage companies with the aptly named 'HaulagePlus Insurance Plan' and 'BuilderPlan Insurance' products.

Zurich, as I said, supplied the marketing content, and, by the way, knowing what I do now, it could have been SO much better! Anyway, we found a list of haulage companies and another for builders, printed the leaflets (they were two-sided leaflets with a tear-off postage paid reply card) and mailed them.

I didn't expect a lot of responses, which would have been okay, because the policies were usually five-figure amounts and as a broker we took a commission of 17.5%. But what happened next has stuck with me ever since.

About five days later, the first replies started coming in and then it was like an avalanche. We got hundreds of replies. We mailed 4000 builders and 2000 haulage companies, and although I can't remember the exact numbers, I believe we received just under 300 responses from the builder leaflet and 200 from the haulage leaflet.

Wow!

A simple two-page leaflet generated around a 10% response.

And remember, none of these firms had ever heard of us. It was the first contact we had ever had with them. Yet they sent the reply-paid cards back the moment they saw them. The other thing to mention here (and again we'll talk more about this later) is that back in the early nineties, the internet hardly existed, so direct mail was one of the very few channels available to reach potential clients, customers or patients.

People were receiving stacks of mail every day, so competition to grab attention was tough ... yet one in ten people responded.

As I said, I know the leaflets weren't the best they could have been, but because they were both focused on specific markets and the policies were aligned to those specific markets, it created an avalanche of leads.

And that's what happens when you identify exactly who you want as your best clients and then tailor your messaging to them.

It's a great lesson.

In fact, it's THE lesson.

When it comes to growing and scaling your established service business, this simple truth is the number-one way to generate results.

In my experience, every service business I've come into contact with fails to clearly identify their Perfect Client Avatar and then match their messaging to it.

People prefer to take a mass-market approach. In other words, they target absolutely everyone who could buy their services rather than focus on the group of people or businesses who are potentially the best possible clients.

I'm sure it's the same for you, too.

Even if you know and understand who your best clients are, in all likelihood you don't laser-beam focus in on them.

Look at all your existing marketing and advertising material. Is it crystal clear who you are targeting, or are you (as I suspect) trying to speak to everyone?

But identifying the Perfect Client Avatar is even more important than you may be thinking.

Why?

Because it sits at the very top of THE MACHINE.

It's the fuel that feeds it.

When you get it right, it's like you're feeding THE MACHINE with the highest grade of premium fuel.

When you get it wrong, it's like putting unleaded fuel into a diesel engine ... it works for a short time but then stops and breaks down.

So, what do you want to feed your business with?

High-grade premium unleaded fuel or diesel?

That's the difference between targeting the right people rather than targeting no one.

I fully appreciate this is not a 'sexy' or exciting strategy to start with, but I can assure you, once you identify your Perfect Client Avatar and use that to fuel YOUR MACHINE, you'll never look back.

And just to emphasise the point ...

Because the Perfect Client Avatar is the fuel for THE MACHINE, everything else – and I mean *everything* else – in THE MACHINE is also completely focused on it. That's why it's so important: it optimises results across the entire system.

So, let's get straight to it ...

Exactly WHO is your Perfect Client Avatar?

This may seem like a pretty obvious question, but as I've said, most people get it wrong. You see, it's important to appreciate that you can't be all things to all people. For example, just because you may have, let's say, a leadership programme for business owners, and you know that most will benefit from your service, it's important you recognise that you need to define who would be your BEST clients.

Not all clients are created equal, and you need to focus on those who have a huge appetite for your area of expertise, can afford it and appreciate what you do for them.

I often see service providers chasing business from people who simply can't afford what it is they're being offered ... which is just a big fat waste of time and money. For you to take your service business to the next level and beyond you must work with clients who can afford your services, are willing to pay you handsomely for the privilege and greatly value what you do for them.

So, let's take the leadership example I just mentioned. People creating a new business start-up would definitely benefit hugely from your expertise and services, but is a brand-new start-up able to pay for your them? It's often better to work with fewer clients paying you more ... than working with a larger number paying you less. And would it be better for you to deliver your leadership programme to specific market segments such as accountants, dentists or any other type of business market? It's your decision, of course, but getting this right now will set you up for incredible success and prevent you from working with the wrong type of clients in the wrong sectors.

Now, of course, we don't live in a perfect world, so not all clients you acquire will be perfect, but if you focus on this now – the majority will be.

You MUST have no doubt who your best type of client is to target them effectively. To do that you first need to create what I call the Perfect Client Avatar Profile.

The Perfect Client Avatar Profile enables you to, figuratively speaking, get inside their heads so you can speak their language and deliver exactly what they want and need in relation to your services and area of expertise. And then you can use the Avatar Profile to target these Perfect Clients, which I'll take you through shortly.

But let's start at the beginning, because I need you to understand why identifying your Perfect Client Avatar is so important before explaining how to create your Avatar Profile.

As I've said, identifying your Perfect Client Avatar is the single most important thing you can do, and let me tell you … and as I said, most people get it horribly wrong!

The common approach that most people adopt is to try and sell their services to everyone, just like the big companies do.

But the big brands spend millions every year to keep their products up front and central to as many people as they can. And of course, people like you and I don't have millions lying around to spend on marketing, do we?

We have to be more strategic, and we can do that by being much more targeted.

In fact, let me show you a short clip to highlight this …

When I saw this film for the first time, I thought it perfectly demonstrated what targeting is.

The clip was an experiment conducted by the Washington Post about a guy called Joshua Bell playing music in a subway in Washington. And if you don't know who Joshua Bell is … and

THE MACHINE

I certainly didn't at the time ... he's one of the leading violinists in the world.

You'll see him busking and playing his violin at the entrance to the subway. Towards the end of the video a question will come up on screen, and I want you to write the answer down.

Simply go to THE MACHINE Resources Page here:

www.themachine.co.uk/book-resources

Then watch the first video ...

Answer the question at the end of the video, then turn the page ...

He made just $32 dollars in change.

That isn't much, is it?

It's not very impressive for a guy who commands a minimum of $5000 a performance.

So, what was the problem?

Well, it's obvious, isn't it ...

First of all, the location and the environment wasn't best suited to classical music ... and secondly his audience were just normal, everyday people going about their business.

It goes to show that unless you target the right people ... you'll earn peanuts! Yes, Joshua did earn money, but it was just a fraction of what he could have made if the people he was playing to were classical music enthusiasts.

Does that make sense?

So, instead of targeting the masses, you need to change and target the people or businesses who are perfect for your service and will pay you handsomely for it.

Let me show you exactly what I mean ...

Traditional Target Everyone (Mass Marketing) Versus Target Marketing

The diagrams in Figures 3.1 and 3.2 show the differences between targeting everyone (mass marketing) and targeting your Perfect Client Avatar (target marketing) ...

The Market Universe
The prospects who could buy your services – Mass Market.

Prospects Who Are Unlikely to Buy
The white space represents potential clients that are unlikely to buy but all receive the same marketing message from you, which results in needless and excessive expense.

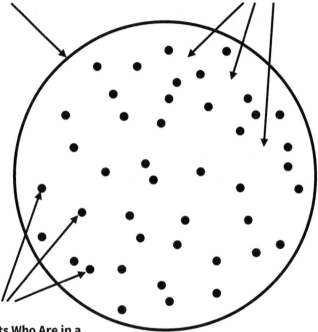

Prospects Who Are in a Position to Buy
Note how disparate these are. The white space in between represents everyone else in the mass market. You have to spend much more money to get 'lucky' and hit the right people/businesses.

The Result
High cost to reach buyers. Response and sales are low, because you're targeting everyone with a 'mass market' message (i.e. it doesn't directly appeal to the buyers).

Figure 3.1. Targeting Everyone: The 'Mass Marketing' Approach

The Market Universe

The prospects who <u>could</u> buy your services – Mass Market.

Prospects Who Are Unlikely to Buy

The white space represents potential clients who are still unlikely to buy but all receive the tailored marketing message from you. Notice there are fewer now!

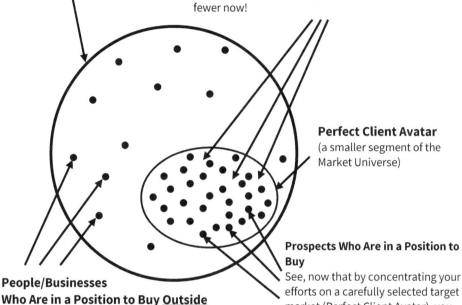

Perfect Client Avatar
(a smaller segment of the Market Universe)

People/Businesses Who Are in a Position to Buy <u>Outside</u> the Perfect Client Avatar

Even this approach isn't perfect, but it's close! You can't hope to 'catch' everyone. There will still be other people/businesses outside the chosen Perfect Client Avatar that you 'miss'. But notice how few there are.

Prospects Who Are in a Position to Buy

See, now that by concentrating your efforts on a carefully selected target market (Perfect Client Avatar), you 'capture' a high proportion of potential buyers. Plus, once you've generated the lead, your message then also needs to be completely focused on this group, so sales are increased significantly.

The Result

This gives you the ability to concentrate your efforts on a more targeted group. The Perfect Client Avatar targeting approach increases the likelihood of a sale and enables YOU to take a big slice of this specific market.

Figure 3.2. The Perfect Client Approach

Multiple Perfect Client Avatars

You don't have to restrict yourself to just one Perfect Client Avatar. You may find it necessary to focus on two or more avatars, depending on the services you provide. For example, an accountant may have three Perfect Client Avatars:

- start-up businesses

- £500,000–£1 million businesses

- £1 million–£2 million businesses

  Or even more defined ('vertical') Avatars:

- dentists

- media companies

- legal

The accountant in this example would need to communicate very differently with each Perfect Client Avatar, because they are so different. A start-up is very different to a business turning over £2 million, for example. If you think about it, it's completely illogical, but that's what people do!

The diagram in Figure 3.3 shows how this looks.

To be clear ... if you try and target everyone, your message has to be vague, which means it will ultimately cost you more to acquire your clients, and many of them won't be of high quality.

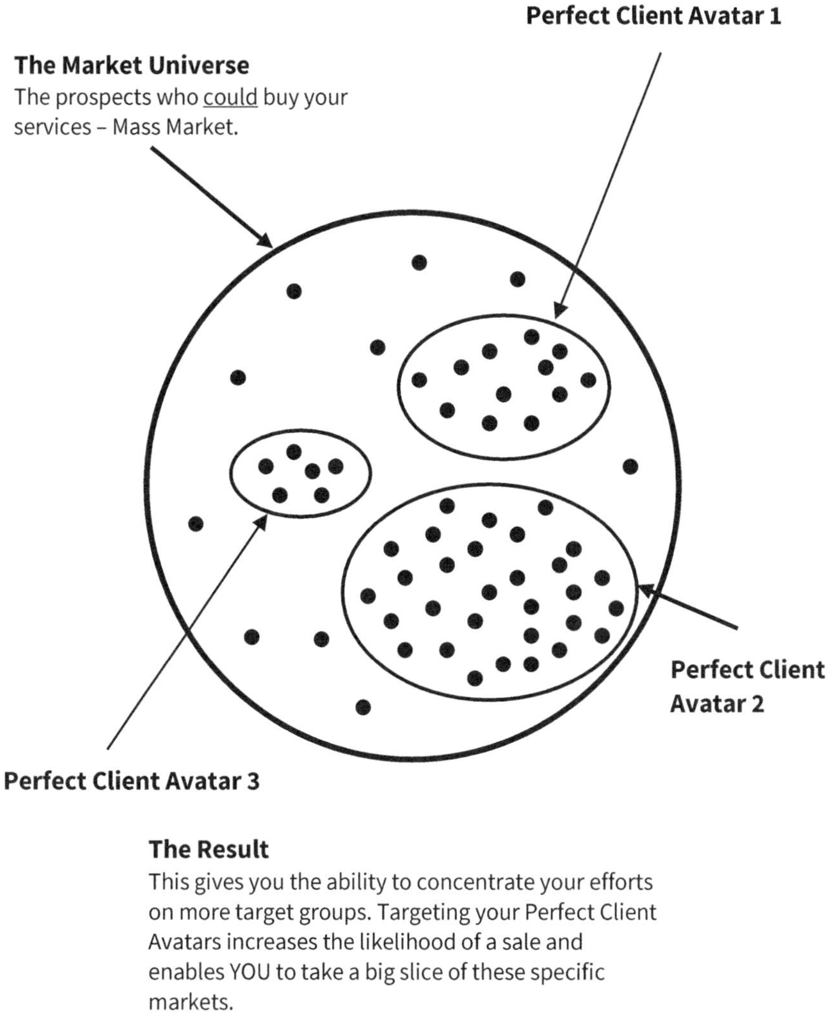

Perfect Client Avatar 1

The Market Universe
The prospects who <u>could</u> buy your services – Mass Market.

Perfect Client Avatar 2

Perfect Client Avatar 3

The Result
This gives you the ability to concentrate your efforts on more target groups. Targeting your Perfect Client Avatars increases the likelihood of a sale and enables YOU to take a big slice of these specific markets.

Figure 3.3. Multiple Perfect Client Avatars

But if you pinpoint a specific market segment(s) by identifying your Perfect Client Avatar(s), then your message can be highly targeted to them, resulting in it costing you far less to acquire clients, and, in the main, those clients will be of a higher quality.

Furthermore, because your message will resonate with them, you'll acquire more of them.

Understanding your Perfect Client Avatar is key, and to illustrate the point I'd like you to watch another video clip.

It's from the film called *What Women Want*, starring Mel Gibson and Helen Hunt, which you may well have seen ... Anyway, it's a great film based on an advertising agency in New York with Gibson playing a 'male chauvinistic pig'.

The agency wants to start to represent female brands, and currently they don't have any. Gibson's character, Nick, has been tasked with trying out some women's brands they're thinking of pitching to take them on as clients.

He reluctantly goes along with it, as he wants to keep his job ... So, back at his apartment, he's trying on lipstick, stockings, hair mousse, and so on, and as he tries to put his foot inside a stocking he slips and falls into the bath which is full of water ... but as he's falling, he knocks the hairdryer off the shelf and it turns on and ends up in the bath too ... and, of course, Gibson gets electrocuted, but as this is a romcom of sorts .... he's miraculously okay.

Anyway, something magical happens, and he wakes up the next day being able to hear what his female cleaner is actually thinking, and he's spooked and thinks he's naturally going mad, so he arranges an appointment with his shrink played by Bette Midler.

The clip starts as Gibson rings her office doorbell ...

Once again, simply go to THE MACHINE Resources Page here:

www.themachine.co.uk/book-resources

Then watch the second video ...

The part right at the end when Bett Midler says to Gibson, 'You must learn from this. If you use it, the world can be yours' is significant.

Just think what that would mean in your service business ... because, if like Mel Gibson ... you knew what your Perfect Client Avatar was thinking ... you could truly build a great business and acquire as many of them as you wanted.

Let me show you how this works ...

Armed with this new confidence, Gibson uses it as he goes to his favourite coffee shop, where he's going to try and get a date with the girl behind the counter, played by Morrisa Tomei.

Now, he's been trying to get a date for months, but he usually goes in all guns blazing without much thought for her feelings.

And he starts exactly like that again, but after hearing what she's thinking, what her fears are, and what her concerns are about dating men ... he quickly changes his approach by tailoring what he says to her.

Let's take a look at what happens.

Watch carefully, because this really is the essence of what can be achieved when you identify and then understand your Perfect Client Avatar ...

Once again, simply go to THE MACHINE Resources Page here:

www.themachine.co.uk/book-resources

Then watch the third video ...

Notice what happened the moment he changed tack and then sympathised with Morrisa. He figuratively speaking joins the conversation going on inside her head, the result being he matches what he says to her thoughts, worries and feelings, and the result, as you saw, was exactly what he wanted – a date with her.

And that's exactly what you can achieve when you identify your Perfect Client Avatar and then tailor your messaging to it.

It makes that much difference.

I hope that makes sense.

So, how do you know what your Perfect Client looks like, thinks about, worries about and all these sorts of things?

THE MACHINE

Well, as I said, you create what I call the Perfect Client Avatar Profile ... and it's really easy to do, which I'll explain shortly.

But first, let me give you a real-world example to put all this into context ...

Let's just say for argument's sake you're starting a new service business and you need an accountant ...

So, you look in your local newspaper, or you type into Google something like 'accountant for start-ups near me'. And let's say you look at the top two Google Ads.

The first ad reads ...

'ABC Chartered Accountants. Tax preparation, auditing, bookkeeping, payroll services and management accounts for all business types'

I think you'll agree this is a typical ad, and it's aimed at the whole business market with a general message.

Most ads you see are like this ... very general.

They're trying to catch everyone, but in fact what they end up doing is catching no one, because the message is so weak and general.

But then compare that to the second ad, which reads ...

XYZ Chartered Accountants specialising in helping service-based business start-ups get their businesses running quickly, profitably and effectively

Look at the difference.

If you've just started a new service business and you're looking for an accountant, I defy you not to at least click on their ad and give XYZ Chartered Accountants a call.

What they're saying is that they *specialise* in working with start-up service businesses.

And that's the key ...

As you can see, these ads are completely different in terms of how they will appeal to a start-up business owner, especially one who is starting a service business.

Obviously, the second one is far more magnetic than the first.

And as I said, it would be very difficult to not click on that ad and then, as long as the page you land on is congruent with the message and it's all about helping start-up service business owners, you are then almost certainly going to contact them. Agreed?

And it's this level of magnetism you must create in your messaging ... and the only way to do that is to first identify the Perfect Client Avatar and then tailor your messaging to it. But how do you do that?

Well, as I mentioned earlier, you create what I call a 'Target Market Avatar Profile' ...

In simple terms this is the exact characteristics of your Perfect Client.

Obviously, there are differences targeting businesses or individuals, but remember, even if you're targeting businesses, you're actually still targeting the individuals in the business as well as the business itself.

There are just six simple steps to creating your Target Market Avatar Profile. Let me take you through each one …

Step #1: Segment Your Existing Client List

What I'm about to take you through is a quick yet very accurate and powerful way to understand your existing client base and draw out the Perfect Clients.

It's a modified version of the Boston Matrix created by the Boston Consulting Group back in the early 1970s.

Over the years I've looked at many models to help established service businesses segment their client base, and all are costly, time consuming and flawed in one way or another.

So, I decided to create my own model … and it will help you segment your client base into four different groups (there is a fifth, and I'll share that with you in a later chapter) and, amongst a number of other notable benefits (which I will explain shortly), will reveal your Perfect Clients.

More importantly, it doesn't cost a single penny and will save you hours and hours.

Of course, the more clients you have, the longer it will take, but even if you have thousands of clients, it will take just one morning for you and your team to go through this modelling process.

Okay, take a look at the Client Segmenting Matrix shown in Figure 3.4 …

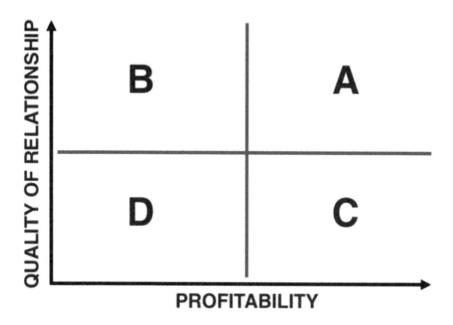

Figure 3.4. The Client Segmenting Matrix

As you can see, there are two axes. The axis along the side is Quality of Relationship. The higher up, the better relationship you have with your clients.

Typically, an excellent relationship with a client means ...

- They treat you and, more importantly, your team with respect.

- They pay their invoices on time.

- They love what you do.

- They appreciate working with you.

- They see the relationship as a partnership.

- They rarely question you on fees.

- And so on.

Lower down the scale the relationship with clients is poor. Typically, this means ...

- They disrespect you or more likely your team (it's rare a client who will treat the owners of your business with disrespect. More likely they will be rude to team members).

- They are always late paying invoices, and accounts have to constantly chase payments.

- They question almost everything you do for them.

- They give the impression that they would rather be working with someone else.

- They see the relationship as supplier/client rather than as a partnership.

- They are always haggling on prices and fees (they may even get alternative quotes from other service providers).

- And so on.

Instinctively, you and your team will know where every client fits on this scale.

Then, the axis along the bottom of the matrix is Profitability. The further to the right, the more profitable a client is. This may take more time to analyse.

You don't need to be forensic with this. My advice is to look at the last 12 months' sales for each client.

Break those sales down into the various services you provide and the average gross profit for each.

Then factor in what I call a *Pain Adjuster*.

This is expressed as a percentage.

So, a client that sits at the top of the Relationship scale gets a weighting of 100%, meaning the gross profit isn't adjusted.

Whereas a client who sits right at the bottom of the Relationship scale gets a weighting of, say, 75%.

If they're somewhere in the middle of the scale, then you'd give them a weighting of, say, 87%.

In other words, because of the 'hassle factor' they bring to your organisation, extra time is spent with them, and it's highly likely you're not factoring this in with them right now.

For example, let's say Client A sits high on the Relationship scale. Their Pain Adjuster is therefore 100%.

Let's also say you provide three different services, and the gross margins on them are 80%, 75% and 70%.

In the last 12 months Client A has spent £20,000 on Service 1 (80% gross profit) and £5000 on Service 3 (70% gross profit).

This is how it looks ...

Client Name	Annual Gross Profit (Service 1)	Annual Gross Profit (Service 2)	Annual Gross Profit (Service 3)	Total Profit	Pain Adjuster	Profitability
A	16,000	0	3500	19,500	100%	19,500

Client B, however, sits low on the Relationship scale. Their Pain Adjuster is therefore 75%.

In the last 12 months Client B has spent £25,000 on Service 1 (80% gross profit) and hasn't taken up Services 2 or 3. This is how it looks ...

Client Name	Annual Gross Profit (Service 1)	Annual Gross Profit (Service 2)	Annual Gross Profit (Service 3)	Total Profit	Pain Adjuster	Profitability
B	20,000	0	0	20,000	75%	15,000

As you can see, in this example, even though Client B has more profit than Client A, after factoring in the Pain Adjuster their profitability reduces to £15,000.

You simply go through each client and work out their profitability based on this model. Don't make it more complicated. This is meant to be a quick and easy way for you to build your own Client Segmentation Matrix.

Now, for each client you have two figures. You have their Pain Adjuster percentage, and you have their Profitability amount.

Your Relationship axis is numbered up to 100%, and your Profitability axis is numbered from the lowest profitability amount up to the highest across your entire client base. So, let's say Client D has the lowest profitability amount of −£1500 (you may lose money on some clients), and Client E has the highest profitability of all clients at £33,000, then your Profitability axis goes from −£1500 to £33,000 (see Figure 3.5) ...

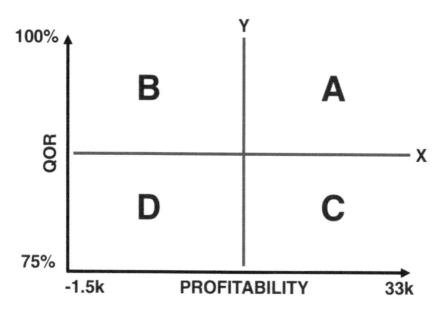

Figure 3.5. Tailored Client Segmenting Matrix

Now, simply plot each client on the matrix. The Matrix above in terms of the four quadrants is divided equally, but you will want to adjust those to best represent your client base.

For example, after allocating the Pain Adjuster to each client, you may well feel that a good client must have a Pain Adjuster above 80%. In effect, that will lower the horizontal line (X).

Again, use your common sense here.

You'll see where each client sits and draw a line just below the client who 'makes the cut' in terms of you seeing them as a decent client with a good relationship. Every client below this line is categorised as having a poor relationship with you.

And then use the same rationale in terms of the profitability for each client. Move the vertical line (Y) either left or right depending on the point you feel is acceptable in terms of profitability. And let's say you set this at £5000 (remember, this is gross profit, so you may feel at £5000, the client isn't great in terms of net profit).

So, your own matrix could look something like the one shown in Figure 3.6.

Now, you know where every client sits.

I'm going to take you through how you use all of the quadrants later in the book to great effect, but for now I want you to simply focus on quadrant A.

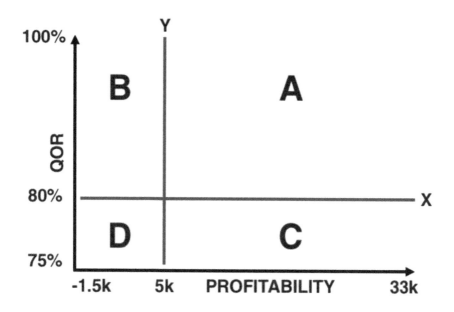

Figure 3.6. Completed Client Segmenting Matrix

As I'm sure you've already figured out, these are your 'Perfect Clients'. These are the clients you're going to use to build your Perfect Client Avatar Profile.

Step #2: Identify Your Perfect Clients' Common Characteristics

Remember, you are now focusing only on clients that are in segment A of your Client Segmenting Matrix.

Now, simply identify their common characteristics.

For example, if you're targeting businesses you'd consider characteristics such as ...

- location

- size in terms of number of employees or turnover

- industry

- products and services they sell

- decision-makers likely to be involved in the purchase of your service and their typical gender and age, etc – if there's more than one decision-maker, it's highly likely they will have different reasons for buying, so make sure you identify each of their character traits

- interests

- what groups they belong to

- and so on ...

You can see how this looks in Figure 3.7.

And then, if you're targeting individuals (consumers) rather than businesses ... you'd consider characteristics such as ...

- type of property, accommodation or dwelling they live in

- age

- gender

- whether they're married or single

- typical income

- location

- hobbies

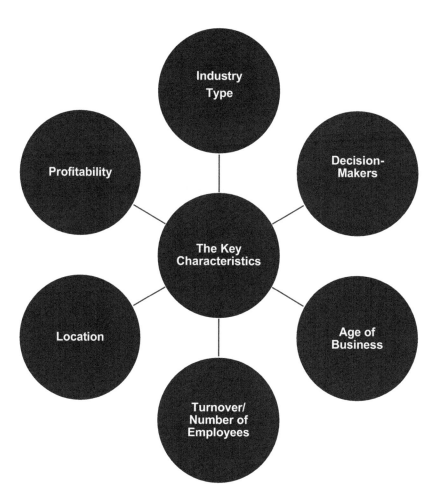

Figure 3.7. Business-to-Business Perfect Client Characteristics

- interests

- type of cars they drive

- what groups they belong to

- other simple demographics such as how many children they have and their ethnicity, and so on.

You can see how this looks in Figure 3.8.

Not all these characteristics will be relevant to you. You just need to think about what characteristics define your Perfect Clients. I promise you, this is easier than you may think.

So, for instance, let's say your expertise is based around diet and exercise, and you sell coaching and mentoring services.

Your Perfect Clients are busy mums who want to lose weight without dieting ...

The characteristics you'd probably want to focus on would be ...

- Obviously, they're female.

- They're overweight or believe they want to lose weight.

- They're aged between 30 and 50.

- They typically have one or more children.

- They're either employed or have their own business.

Figure 3.8. Business-to-Consumer Perfect Client Characteristics

- They live in an owner-occupied detached home with a mortgage.

- The household income is over £40,000.

- And so on.

Notice how already, just by identifying the characteristics, you're automatically starting to create a very well-defined group of people ... but you don't stop there. We can refine it further ...

Step #3: Identify the Motivations for Buying Your Service

There are numerous motivations people have for buying. You just need to identify which apply to your Perfect Clients when they're buying your services.

Here's a list along with a short description of 22 primary motivations in alphabetical order ...

1. Addiction. This is outside the range of the normal human operating system, but it certainly exists and accounts for more sales than any of us can fathom. For example, this is the reason the tobacco industry is so huge the world over.

2. Affiliation. Something that helps bond you to a cultural, religious or community affiliation.

3. Basic Need. We buy things to fulfil what Maslow describes as the bottom of his hierarchy; things such as food and shelter. Many services fulfil this motivation.

4. Celebrity Alignment. People like to have the same things as their favourite celebrity uses. That's why celebrity endorsement works so well.

5. Compulsory Purchase. Many services have to be purchased by businesses or individuals. For example, services such as accounting for businesses and plumbing services for individuals.

6. Convenience. You need something now and will take the easiest or fastest path to get it. Think about the last time you were thirsty and found the nearest type of drink you could. This could also be choosing the safe supplier (no one ever gets fired for hiring IBM), or purchasing something to increase comfort or efficiency.

7. Ego Stroking. Sometimes you make a purchase to impress/attract the opposite sex; to have something bigger/better than others, friends, neighbours, etc.; to look like an expert/aficionado; to meet a standard of social status, often exceeding what's realistically affordable to make it at least seem like you operate at a higher level.

8. Emergency Purchase. When you need services in an emergency (electrician services, appliance repairs, lock repairs, etc.).

9. Empathy. Sometimes people buy from other people because they listened to them and cared about them, even if they had the lesser-value alternative.

10. Event. When the social decorum of an event (e.g., wedding, anniversary, birthday, etc.) dictates buying something.

11. <u>Fear.</u> Many services are purchased out of fear. That doesn't necessarily mean buying things such as protection services; it could be fear of loss (the service could sell out), or the service is such an important one to the buyer that they would do anything to get it and would never risk not being able to get it – one of the most powerful motivations.

12. <u>Fad or Innovation.</u> Some people (not everyone) want the latest and greatest (it's why each version of the iPhone causes hysteria amongst many).

13. <u>Giving.</u> People feel better about themselves by feeling as though they're giving to others, especially when they're promised something in return. Buying things they don't need – or wouldn't normally purchase – because it will help another person or make the world a better place comes under this category.

14. <u>Great Value.</u> When the perceived value substantially exceeds the price of a service. I'm going to talk more about this later when we discuss *irresistible offers.*

15. <u>Indulgence.</u> Who doesn't deserve a bit of luxury now and then? So long as you can afford it (or even if you can't!), sometimes there's no better justification for that hour-long massage, or makeover.

16. <u>Lower Prices.</u> A service you wanted previously but couldn't afford is now cheaper.

17. <u>Name Recognition.</u> When purchasing a category you're unfamiliar with, branding plays a big role. Think of the first-time purchases you've made over the years and how many of those were influenced by advertising.

18. Peer Pressure. Something is purchased because your friends want you to – often happens in teen years.

19. Prestige or Aspirational Purchase. Something is bought for an esteem-related reason or for personal enhancement.

20. Reciprocity. This happens when somebody, gives or buys you something of value or does something exceptionally nice and/or unnecessary. Now, it's your turn to return the favour at the next opportunity. This is known as the 'Law Of Reciprocity', and I'll discuss more on this later (it's a very powerful tool).

21. Replacement. Sometimes you buy because you need to replace your existing service. This could be moving to a superior or better service provider (changing from one lawyer to another, for example).

22. Scarcity. This could be based around limited availability of a particular service (and, as you'll see later, you'll use scarcity to help improve sales).

Write down all those that apply.

Step #4: Identify Your Perfect Clients' Key Pain Points

Pain points are basically the reasons WHY your Perfect Clients buy your services. For example, efficiency, ease of use, time saving, and so on.

Write them all down.

Step #5: Identify the Common Objections

Common objections are basically the reasons why your Perfect Clients DON'T buy.

For example, cost, time, never heard of you before, other alternatives, and so on.

Again, write them all down.

Step #6: Where You Can Find Them (Where Do They 'Hang Out')?

Write down where you can easily reach your Perfect Clients. You'll already have a good idea of this. For example, do they hang out on Facebook, LinkedIn and so on. Are they members of any associations? Can you reach them at home or in their business? What websites do they often visit? Do they read any particular magazines? (Contrary to popular belief the magazine industry is still thriving.)

And once you've done that, you'll have created the Perfect Client Avatar Profile for your service business.

To help you, I've developed a simple Perfect Client Avatar Profile Checklist. You can download it from here:

www.themachine.co.uk/book-resources

Don't underestimate the power of this, because, as I've said, if you don't know who your Perfect Clients are … it's very difficult to tailor your messages to them and almost impossible to know where to find them … and the result is you'll struggle to acquire mentoring clients and do it cost-effectively.

As an example, this is the Perfect Client Avatar Profile we created, when targeting accountants for our accountancy marketing network ...

Common Characteristics:

Industry. Accounting/CPA (not bookkeepers).

Business Type. Owner managed, single site, NOT home office.

Business Size. Sole practitioner and up to four partners maximum.

Decision-Makers. Partners who are entrepreneurial, ambitious, willing to work hard to achieve results, serious about genuinely helping their clients grow better businesses. Frustrated at their growth. Likely to be sceptical because they've tried numerous programmes before and they didn't deliver.

Location. UK and Ireland, USA, Canada, Australia, New Zealand, South Africa.

Motivations for Buying:

- Prestige or Aspirational Purchase (the programme was created to increase their sales and recurring-fee income, as well as help the client personally with their own development).

- Fear (we structured the programme so that only one firm in any one area could join the programme, so we used the fear of missing out).

- Scarcity (only one firm in any one area could join).

- Affiliation (being part of a large group of like-minded accountants).

Key Pain Points:

- Need to get more clients (quality clients).

- Need to increase recurring-fee income.

- Need to maximise value from existing clients.

- Find it hard to convert leads into new clients at the right fee.

- Pressured by low-price competition, online accountants and commodity selling.

- Frightened of the 'Big 4' taking a slice of the action.

- Worried about the impact of online accounting systems such as Xero.

Common Objections:

- Don't trust it will work for them.

- They've tried something 'similar' before, and it didn't generate results.

- Risk of exposing clients to something that didn't deliver.

Where Can You Find Them?

- In and at their business.

- AccountingWEB and other big accounting platforms.

- Accounting Associations (ACCA, ICAEW, CPAA, etc.)

- LinkedIn, Google.

Hopefully, you can now see how these six steps of the Perfect Client Avatar Profile really help you focus on your Perfect Clients. And just like Mel Gibson in the clip you saw, you'll be able to figuratively speaking get inside their heads and create compelling and laser-beam, targeted messages that are magnetic to them.

And because you can do that, as I've already said, your marketing becomes much more focused.

It means you can spend less to reach these people. And it means once you get inside their heads, anything and everything is possible.

And, as you'll discover later in the book, armed with your Perfect Client Avatar Profile you'll be able to laser-beam target the right people or businesses, because no matter what tactics you use to generate leads as part of your Lead Generation System, you'll use this information to pinpoint them with incredible accuracy.

I can't emphasise enough how valuable this is to you.

I promise you, when you get this right, everything else we're going to be doing with THE MACHINE becomes so much easier and more effective. You'll use your Avatar Profile as we go through each of the following chapters.

Chapter Summary and Action Points

- From today onwards, the entire focus of your service business must be on your Perfect Clients!

- To identify your Perfect Clients, go through the six steps of creating the Perfect Client Avatar Profile.

- You'll use the Perfect Client Avatar Profile as the premium grade fuel for your MACHINE.

CHAPTER 4

SELLING THE INVISIBLE: PRODUCTISING YOUR SERVICES

My first business, which, if you recall, I started when rugby union turned professional, was a marketing consultancy. But, of course, back then I was inexperienced, wet behind the ears and learning my craft. Consequently, I made a huge number of mistakes.

Fortunately, though, very early on I was lucky enough to meet a very interesting prospective client.

He had built one of the UK's most successful firms of lawyers, with offices all over the country. He had been drawn to me from an ad I'd placed in a very large publication called the *Solicitors Gazette* here in the UK.

I took him through my proposal for working with him and his firm, and he turned around to me and said something like, 'Steve, thanks for coming to see me today. I like what you're doing, but I can't really see what it is you're selling. Also, there are numerous consultants selling what you're selling; you're not unique. You're also selling a service which, by its nature, is hard for people to appreciate what it can do for them. One of the reasons why we've been so successful is that we've made our legal services sound and feel like products. They all have specific names unique to us. They all have systems of delivery. They all have features and benefits. You're trying to sell me the result, which is what I want, but I can't see how you're going to achieve that.'

Needless to say, I didn't acquire them as clients, but that meeting was the catalyst to immediately make my services more *tangible* and was a painful reminder of the valuable lesson that I had previously learned from the large insurance brokers ... and forgotten!

You see, we are selling the invisible. As you know, services by their nature can't be seen or touched. They don't smell. They have no volume or weight. And that, as you know, makes them far more difficult to sell than a physical product.

Products, as I mentioned earlier, are so much easier to sell.

Many have unique features and benefits. Someone can enter a market and create an avalanche of sales simply because their product is different and new, and has additional features and benefits that no others have.

And, as you already have an established service business, you've already found a way to sell your services, but if you transform your services into a product, or at least make them 'feel' more like a product, you can be so much more successful.

I call this transformation: *Productising Your Services.*

Productising Your Services is THE most effective way I know to ...

- sell, them more easily than you do already;

- differentiate and position them away from your competition (so you win more business);

- create price elasticity (gives you the ability to charge more for your services);

- avoid direct comparison (so you avoid commodity buying and can maintain or increase your pricing).

There are three elements to Productising Your Services. I call this the Service Transformation Triangle (STT), as shown in Figure 4.1.

Let me take you through it ...

STT Element #1: Name Your Service

This first element alone, when you get it right, can increase sales.

Key to the name, though, is not to use any industry jargon! Use a name that is easily understood by your Perfect Clients. A name that is completely different to anything else out there when it comes to the services of your competition.

Virtually everyone in the service industry has a list of services, and, irrespective of the supplier you go to, the services are all pretty much named the same.

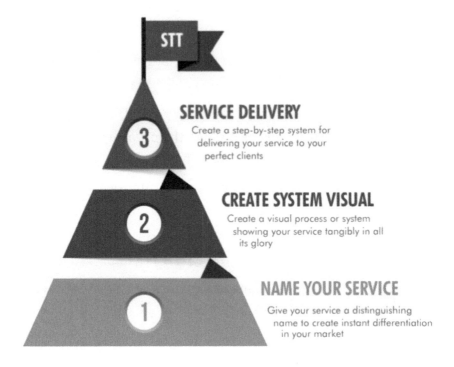

Figure 4.1. The Service Transformation Triangle (STT)

Using accounting as an example, and I could take any industry to demonstrate this, every firm uses the industry-led terms for the names of their services.

For example ...

- Tax Planning
- Management accounts
- VAT and PAYE Review
- Managing Your Wealth
- Exit Planning
- Raising Finance
- Budgets and Forecasts

Selling The Invisible: Productising Your Services

These services are listed and discussed by every accountant on the planet, and when that happens you turn even a highly professional industry into a commodity-based one, because if the client believes they can get the same service from somewhere else, then price ultimately wins (why pay for the same service if you can get it cheaper elsewhere?).

With a little thought, all these service types can be given unique and compelling service names:

- Tax Planning becomes 'ProfitSafe – keeping Your Money In Your Hands'

- Management accounts becomes 'Business Performance Tracker – Monitoring the Health of Your Business'

- VAT and PAYE Review becomes 'The Sleep-Easy – Business Compliance Security'

- Managing Your Wealth becomes The Whole Point – Keeping What's Yours'

- Exit Planning becomes 'FutureSafe – Planning For Your Business Exit'

- Raising Finance becomes 'Business Builder – Raising Investment and Funds for Your Growth'

- Budgets and Forecasts becomes 'Decision-Maker – Looking to the Future to Aid Your Decision-Making Today'

Do you see how easy this is?

Here are some more examples of service names from my own businesses and clients ...

- *THE MACHINE* (the name we give to the service to help established service businesses to grow, scale and jump to the next level and beyond).

- *Sales Accelerator Programme* (the name we give to the coaching and mentoring service our mentors use to help the owners of small businesses to grow and increase their profits).

- *AssetOne Wealth System* (the name one of our clients use for the service they deliver to help people become property millionaires within three years).

- *High-Net-Worth, Iron-Fortress Security Blueprint* (the name one of our clients uses for the service they deliver to help protect the lives, businesses and assets of their VIP and ultra-high-net-worth clients).

- *The Gameplan* (the name one of our clients uses for the service they deliver to help create high-performing teams in businesses with large teams of people).

- *Coach Me Slim and Trim* (the name one of our clients uses for the service they deliver to help busy women over 40 to lose weight and keep it off).

As an important aside, to add an extra layer of copyright protection and value to your service name you can also get the name trademarked.

Notice that these service names immediately differentiate all these businesses from everyone else in the market sectors they work in. It's impossible to compare like for like, especially when the process or system diagram is added to it, which leads me nicely on to the second element …

STT Element #2: Create System Visual

The reality is that you already have a system that you use to deliver your service to your clients. All you have to do now is bring it to life by writing down the high-level steps of that system and then make it visual so your Perfect Clients can see it.

For example, when it came to creating the system diagram for THE MACHINE, the seven high-level elements of it were already created …

- The Perfect Client Avatar
- Productising the Services
- Lead Generation System
- Conversion System
- Maximising Client Value System
- Automation
- Scaling Up

Next, I just needed to decide how to visually display them working together as part of an entire system.

There are numerous ways of doing this. You can use pie charts, diagrams and illustrations that simply show your Perfect Clients how the high-level elements fit together.

With THE MACHINE, we use the simple diagram you're already familiar with to show it (see Figure 4.2).

The AssetOne Wealth System is a pie chart (see Figure 4.3).

And the 'High-Net-Worth, Iron-Fortress Security Blueprint' is an illustration (see Figure 4.4).

All these types of visuals work very well to demonstrate your service system and transform it into a 'product'. You can create your visual yourself or ask a graphic designer to do it for you.

In two steps you've taken an intangible service and changed it into a 'product' that no other competitor has. You've made it incomparable. You've taken it away from a commodity type service into a value-based service. You've created a differentiator, and it's cost you absolutely nothing to do it.

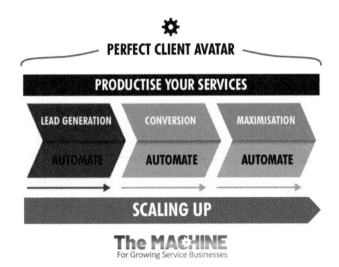

Figure 4.2. THE MACHINE

Figure 4.3. The AssetOne Wealth System

Figure 4.4. The High-Net-Worth, Iron-Fortress Security Blueprint

The last part of the STT is to then create a delivery system ...

STT Element #3: Service Delivery

Elements 1 and 2 are key to Productising Your Services, and do it with zero or little cost. Element 3 ties them together to make sure you deliver your service to your Perfect Clients in the best way possible.

I cover this in much more detail in Chapter 13 (Scaling Up Part 3: Systems, Systems, Systems), but for now, be mindful of the fact that by Productising Your Services, you will almost certainly have improved and modified what you were doing previously.

In fact, one of the 'hidden' benefits of going through this process is that it really gets you thinking clearly about the system you use to deliver your services to clients. And because of that, you will make significant improvements as you go.

*****

Okay, you're cooking on gas now. You've identified your Perfect Client Avatar and created your Avatar Profile, and you've Productised Your Services. You're now armed with everything you need to implement and optimise the rest of THE MACHINE, and that's what we'll focus on now ...

Chapter Summary and Action Points

- Transforming your service into a product is a very important part of building your business and taking it to the next level.

- There are three elements to Productising Your Services ...

  ELEMENT #1: Name Your Service
  ELEMENT #2: Create System Visual
  ELEMENT #3: Service Delivery

- Once you've Productised Your Services you've instantly differentiated them from your competition and moved away from commodity type selling into value-based selling, and as a result you'll acquire more clients at the right fee.

THE MACHINE

CHAPTER 5

THE GROWTH CONTINUUM

In all my years working with businesses across hundreds of different sectors and markets, the biggest failing I see in terms of their development is that they don't focus on EVERY growth area of their business.

Yet it's not their fault!

You see, the focus of almost every marketing and digital agency tends to be around generating leads. Most gurus talk about the importance of generating leads and how to do it. Online courses also focus heavily on lead generation.

And although lead generation is, of course, absolutely vital, it's just one part of what I call the *Growth Continuum*.

There are, in fact, three growth areas in every business …

1. Lead Generation (generating Perfect Client leads).

2. Conversion (converting as many of those leads into clients at the right fee).

3. Maximising Client Value (retaining clients and increasing sales and profits from them).

As I said, most of the focus is on lead generation, and very little time and attention is dedicated to conversion and maximising client value.

That's a huge mistake, because, as you know, lead generation is by far the most costly of the three growth areas. In fact, conversion and maximising client value cost very little, no matter how small or large your business is, and no matter what services you sell.

What's also interesting is that maximising client value automatically and seamlessly follows conversion, which automatically and seamlessly follows lead generation. In other words, they are inextricably linked to each other.

That's why I call all three the Growth Continuum.

And although most established service businesses have some kind of effort on all three growth areas, it's extremely rare that they are systemised and working to their maximum with many thousands simply left on the table.

The arrow on the right shown in Figure 5.1 shows where the Growth Continuum sits in THE MACHINE.

Each of the three growth areas has a series of consecutive steps. These steps make up the system for each of the growth areas. It's highly likely that once you have implemented the three systems into your business you will have between 30 and 50 individual steps making up the Growth Continuum.

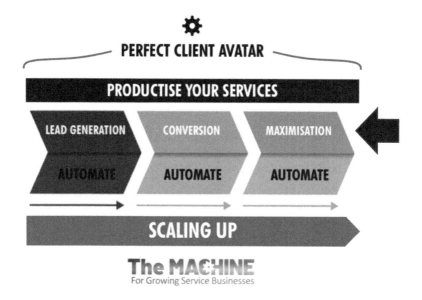

Figure 5.1. Where the Growth Continuum Sits in THE MACHINE

And it's to each of these 30 to 50 steps that we apply the process known as 'Marginal Gains', which I'll cover with you in Chapter 12, Scaling Up Part 2, The Science of Marginal Gains.

Even though I obviously don't know anything about your service business, I can be confident that you are not utilising all three growth areas, and I'd be even more surprised if you had a system for each. Even of you have, they can all be significantly improved.

As a result, huge gains can be made in your business.

When I'm working with our clients, the Growth Continuum, with its three growth systems, is so important that we dedicate a whole day together in a luxury hotel so that we can map out every step across it.

It's an amazing day that shapes the future of their businesses ... and during the next three chapters I'm going to help you do the same ...

Chapter Summary and Action Points

- There are three, not one, growth areas in every business ...

  GROWTH AREA #1: Lead Generation
  GROWTH AREA #2: Conversion
  GROWTH AREA #3: Maximising Client Value

- All three growth areas are made up of a series of consecutive steps to create three interlinked systems.

- The three growth systems combine to create the Growth Continuum.

CHAPTER 6

LEAD GENERATION SYSTEM

Most service businesses have a real challenge when it comes to generating a constant flow of leads. It's highly likely you're not generating enough leads right now for your own service business. You're probably missing a system that predictably generates leads for you 24/7, 365 days a year. Right?

Remember, when it comes to THE MACHINE, it's your Lead Generation System that feeds the Growth Continuum ...

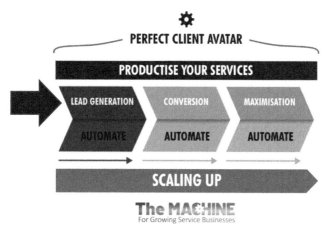

THE MACHINE

But imagine if you had a system in place that worked tirelessly night and day, even while you were asleep or on holiday, a system that produced high-quality leads from your Perfect Clients. That would be something, wouldn't it?

Well, the good news is that is absolutely possible. However, you're going to have to change how you've been doing things.

To take your service business to the next level requires a Lead Generation System that once in place will produce a level of lead flow that you never thought possible.

Even if you're selling a high-ticket service worth thousands, this system will ensure you generate a constant stream of leads from your Perfect Clients.

Better still, the system I'm going to show you, will never go out of date (it's been working for decades) and once in place produces a conveyor belt of leads ready for you to convert into clients (you'll have a system for this, too).

From now on, you need to see your Lead Generation System as a series of steps, a series of logical steps that are in place to maximise the number of high-quality leads and minimise the cost to acquire those leads (cost per lead).

And before I take you through the system, you also need to change your thinking on lead generation. Even though lead flow is important, the key number is 'cost per lead'. This is the number that will drive your decision-making, but more on that shortly.

Figure 6.1 shows the Lead Generation System. As you can see, it has four key steps ...

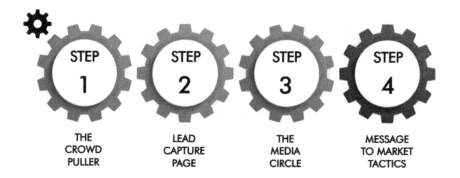

Figure 6.1. The Lead Generation System

Let me take you through it, step by step ...

Step #1: THE CROWD PULLER

The most important job you have when it comes to generating leads is to grab the ATTENTION of your Perfect Clients.

If you fail at this first step (as most service businesses do!), then your Lead Generation System will always be broken.

Attention is ALL THAT MATTERS.

It's been the same for hundreds of years, and it will continue for hundreds of years to come.

But the good news is that once you've clearly identified your Perfect Clients and created the Perfect Client Avatar Profile, you're then equipped to grab the attention of those Perfect Clients and pull them towards you.

And you do that with a '**Crowd Puller**'.

A Crowd Puller is an asset that magnetically draws your Perfect Clients to you in vast numbers, something that is highly desirable to them, something that also demonstrates your expertise.

The Crowd Puller achieves all these things and more.

I'll shortly reveal the three most powerful Crowd Pullers, but first I want to explain the concept behind what makes a successful Crowd Puller and one that your Perfect Clients simply can't ignore when they see it.

I call this concept 'Expertise First'.

Here's what it is and why it works so well ...

Expertise First

I learned this concept while I was playing rugby for Leicester Tigers.

Back in early 1997, a huge new industry was about to be born in world sport. It was called SAQ – Speed, Agility and Quickness. It was developed by Randy Smyth. Randy was a US 100-metre sprinter. He never quite made the US Olympic team, but he was fascinated by the human body and how it could be 'taught' to run faster and become more agile.

Quietly, he had been developing a number of techniques and patented training aids, and was working with a number of American football athletes, basketball players, baseball players and sprinters. His results were phenomenal.

He had taken the traditional speed and agility techniques that had been around for decades and built an entire range of products to shortcut the process of being able to run quicker and become more agile.

The problem he had was that no one (except his small group of athletes) had ever heard of SAQ or Speed City (Randy's original company).

So, he decided he had to show people how it all worked (Expertise First).

He created the first-ever SAQ Super Conference. It was held in New Orleans in January 1997. Prior to the launch of the Super Conference, he had reached out to a number of agents across the English-speaking world that he had built relationships with over the years and asked them to source the fastest athletes in each country with a view to them becoming ambassadors for him and SAQ.

Back in 1997 I was one of the fastest rugby players in the UK, and I received a call from Randy's UK agent (Alan Pearson), who had already been in touch with Leicester Tigers and, along with one of the Tigers' coaching team (former Australian second row Duncan Hall), I was given permission by the Club to be the UK ambassador for SAQ.

But before agreeing to do that, Randy invited us over to the Super Conference to see what the fuss was all about. During the three-day conference, Randy took all these world-famous coaches and athletes in dozens of different sports across dozens of countries through all his techniques. He didn't ask anyone to pay a penny to attend.

In the back of his mind, he knew that once he showed the coaches and athletes the techniques, training aids and training programmes, he would instantly create the desire for his services and products. And boy was he right!

That single conference launched a new and radical training concept that revolutionised the speed and agility industry. Actually, to be accurate, there wasn't even an industry before Randy. He created it.

And he created it using the concept I now call *Expertise First*.

Once Randy showed his expertise to his Perfect Clients (professional coaches and athletes), with their support he knew people would find it virtually impossible for them to NOT buy his services, products and programmes. And he was right.

Although most people aren't aware of this, Randy was the man who created the entire SAQ industry, and now his techniques and products are used by professional and amateur sports at all ages. If you have children and you see them running in between 'ladders' or jumping over small 'hurdles' and other speed and agility aids, the likelihood is they were all originally born out of Randy's Speed City.

Although I wouldn't use this concept for some years, Randy's SAQ conference made an indelible mark on me, especially the power of Expertise First. I can tell you that after that conference not one person had any doubts about Randy's expertise .... but if he'd simply tried to sell his programmes and training aids first, rather than demonstrating his expertise, he would never have created such a successful international business, let alone within a three-day period!

You can apply this concept to EVERY business, but, of course, as a service provider, Expertise First is an even more valuable and powerful concept.

To reinforce this, I can tell you I've tried numerous ways to generate leads and clients ... and Expertise First beats anything else by a landslide.

Ultimately, if you can demonstrate your expertise to your Perfect Clients *prior* to selling your services, prospects are far more likely to become clients. In fact, I'd go as far as to say that if you get this right, you'll never, ever have to worry about where the next client will come from.

The best way to demonstrate this, is by using a **FREE** Crowd Puller, as Randy did with his SAQ Super Conference.

I call this an *Expertise First Crowd Puller*. So, Randy's Super Conference was his Expertise First Crowd Puller. But you definitely don't need to go to the extremes or costs that Randy did.

Your Expertise First Crowd Puller can take the form of many different things, but by far the BEST three Expertise First Crowd Pullers are as follows ...

1. FREE Special Report

2. FREE Webinar/On-Demand Training

3. FREE Book

Each one of these Expertise First Crowd Pullers works very hard to grab the ATTENTION of your Perfect Clients.

Let me take you quickly through each one ...

1. FREE Special Report

When I created my first system, The POWER Marketing System For Service Businesses, I knew I needed something that would first grab the attention of my Perfect Clients.

As I mentioned earlier, by this time I'd already experienced Randy's Super Conference and why that free event worked so well (Expertise First).

So, I decided to create my first-ever Special Report.

It was a 24-page report that explained how I could help any service business owner to grow their business using the POWER Marketing System.

Figure 6.2 shows the first page of the report (look, I even had a little bit of hair back then!).

By creating the Special Report, I could simply promote the virtues of the free report to my Perfect Clients.

Then, once they read it, the report would demonstrate my expertise, and then and only then was I able to sell the system to them (the report did that over the last six pages).

It was the perfect Crowd Puller, and it worked like a charm here in the UK.

"How To Quickly, Easily
And Consistently Grow Your
Service Business With Big
Profits"

From the desk of Steve Hackney

Hi, my name is Steve Hackney, and as I mentioned in my ad that you answered, I'm a marketing guy who has created a very successful, almost foolproof process to grow service businesses.

In your heart you know you are an expert in your field. That's important. You know you can help people solve their problems. You feel you deserve to be making more money - after all you know your stuff!

Have you ever said this to yourself or to your partner?...

**"We're really good! If we could only get more
clients and more money from existing clients we'd
be rolling in it!"**

You know what?

**EVEN THE GREATEST SERVICE PROVIDER IN THE WORLD WILL
GO BROKE WITHOUT A CONSTANT STREAM OF NEW CLIENTS AND
REGULAR INCOME FROM EXISTING CLIENTS!**

You see, selling services (as I'm sure you're aware) is very different and much more challenging than selling products. It requires a very different approach. **AND THAT'S THE PROBLEM!**

Let me explain...

(next page please...)

- 1 -

Figure 6.2. My Original Expertise First Crowd Puller

Then, as the internet's growth became more established, it meant I could expand the business internationally, and I created my second FREE Special Report titled, 'The 27 Common Marketing Mistakes That Right Now Are Costing Service-Based

107

Businesses Millions Each Year'. Figure 6.3 shows the front page of it ...

Figure 6.3. My Second Expertise First Crowd Puller

And since the early 2000s, using a FREE Special Report that's available online is the way to do it because of the automation you can bring to the system, which I'll talk about later.

The primary aim of your Special Report is, of course, to demonstrate you are an expert. But remember, it MUST be focused on your Perfect Clients.

This is why you have to create your Perfect Client Avatar Profile FIRST. Everything – and I mean *everything* – MUST be tailored to your Perfect Clients so it resonates with them at a much higher level.

To decide on the content of the report, simply ask yourself the following question ...

'What information relating to my service and my expertise would be useful for my Perfect Clients to read about?'

Here are some good examples ...

- Accountant – improving cash flow.

- Garden care – how to eliminate weeds and create a beautiful lush green lawn.

- Structural Engineer – the effects of trees on buildings (when targeting architects).

- Martial Arts – using martial arts to mould 'perfect children'.

- Overseas property services – legal issues and loopholes.

- Carpet Fitter – cleaning the carpet so it looks brand new, even after ten years.

- Printer – saving money on print formats.

- Graphic Designer – designing a brochure that generates sales.

- Lawyer/Solicitor – what to think about before going through a divorce.

- Marketing Consultant – using YouTube advertising.

- Recruitment Specialist – interview techniques.

- Insurance Broker – reducing risk.

- Training company – effective leadership skills.

It is quite easy to think of dozens of subject areas for your own service. If you are struggling to come up with anything yourself, have a brainstorming session with a colleague. Another way of doing this, which again is very successful, is to create your report around this template ...

'What Every _____ (insert your Perfect Client Avatar) Should Know Before Working with a _____ (insert your service sector)'.

Once you know the content of your report, THE most important element is your TITLE.

It's the title that grabs the attention of your Perfect Clients.

... and the content demonstrates your expertise.

But if you don't grab your Perfect Clients' attention, then no matter how good your content is, people simply won't read it, because they won't want the report!

If the prospect dismisses your report title, that's it; you've lost them, and you won't get them as a lead.

Your title can be the difference between success and failure; it's that important.

Here are a couple of successful titles that we've used for Special Reports ...

Marketing Consultant

57 Golden Ways to Multiply Your Online Results

Lawyer/Solicitor (family law)

17 Common Divorce Mistakes and How to Avoid Them

Security

7 Security Secrets Used by Royalty and Heads of State to Create an 'Iron Fortress' Around Their Family, Assets and Businesses

Accountant

15 Proven Ways to Increase Your Profits Without Spending a Penny

Graphic Designer

How to Design a Website to Get Results

Carpet Fitter and Supplier

Caring for Your Carpets So They Keep Their Beauty and Last Longer

Then, simply write the report (it will take you around 4–8 hours, that's all).

Make sure the front page of the report looks professional and is in keeping with your Perfect Clients.

We almost always get a graphic designer to create the front page, but if you do, ensure they adhere to the following ...

- The title of the report must stand out. That's achieved using big letters, using upper and lower case.

- Imagery should reinforce the title of the report.

- Branding/logo should be small and not dominate the cover.

This is very important, because as you'll see when we get onto Step #4 (Lead Capture Page), the cover is your 'hero shot' (the primary image on the page) and becomes a key part of the page.

Figures 6.4, 6.5 and 6.6 show good examples of how design based around these simple guidelines can create a stunningly visual cover.

The last but most important element of your Special Report is your 'Call to Action'.

Your Call to Action is simply telling the reader what to do next.

In other words, you want them to move to the first step of your Conversion System, which we'll cover in detail in the next Chapter.

Your Call to Action comes at the end of the Special Report, naturally flowing on from your content (see example in the next chapter).

The Top 10 Security Protocols
Royalty And Heads Of State Use
To Create An 'Iron Fortress' Around
Their Family, Assets & Businesses

...And How You Can Use Them Too!

DJR SECURITY
AND RISK MANAGEMENT

Figure 6.4. Perfectly Designed Special Report Front Cover

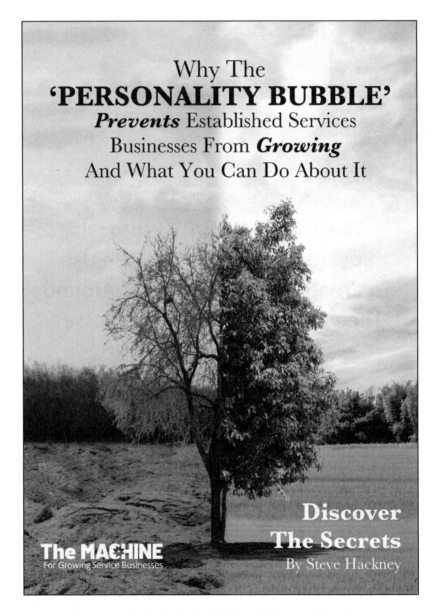

Figure 6.5. Perfectly Designed Special Report Front Cover

Figure 6.6. Perfectly Designed Special Report Front Cover

2. FREE Webinar/On-Demand Training

My advice for you is to first create your Special Report. There are just a small number of moving parts, and the entire process is simple:

1. Create report.

2. Download report.

3. Read report.

There's a little more to it than that, which I'll explain in the next chapter, but that is essentially it. That's why I love Special Reports.

On the other hand, free webinars and on-demand training are more complicated. There are a lot of moving parts. However, they are an excellent Expertise First Crowd Puller, because you have more time to deliver your content, and you're delivering it personally to them (rather than in written form).

I've been delivering webinars since 2009, and I've seen a lot of changes since then, but they continue to be an excellent way to sell services, from low- to high-ticket and across any industry.

In fact, they have been our number-one method to sell our membership programmes and high-value services such as our 'Done-For-You Client Programme' and, of course, are major players in our clients' successes, too.

The difference between a webinar and on-demand training is simply that webinars require your Perfect Clients to select a date and time to tune in to your webinar, whereas on-demand training, delivers the same great content except the training is available pretty much immediately (within ten minutes).

This is not the platform to take you through all the steps required to create a webinar or on-demand training, but I do go through all the key steps and stages in my book *Business Mentoring Success*.

I have also created step-by-step training on creating webinars called Webinar Success.

The image in Figure 6.7 shows the high-level stages of creating a successful webinar ...

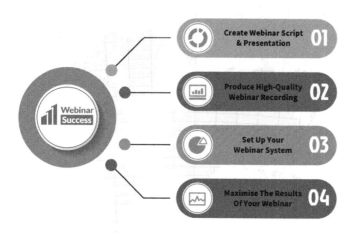

Figure 6.7. The High-Level Stages of Webinar Success

Just one point to note here: I do not advocate you run live webinars as part of your Lead Generation System. That's not scalable. You need to automate them, so you record your webinar once and then use automation software to run it on autopilot. I'll explain how this is done in Chapter 9: Putting It All on Autopilot.

3. FREE Book

The third Crowd Puller is without question the one which will deliver the best results for you.

Having your own book is, of course, the best Expertise First Crowd Puller. That's because not only is it full of your expertise, but people also automatically assume that because you're an author, you're an expert on the subject area of your book.

Of course, that's true – you are!

The other reason why a book is so successful (and it's the same with your Special Report and webinar/on-demand training) is that few, if any of your competitors, will have written a book, so you gain further distinction in your market.

Along with free reports and webinars, my books have helped us quickly gain huge volumes of clients in the sectors that we have operated in.

For example, when we launched into the accountancy market, I co-authored the book with Richard Brewin titled, *How to Quickly Grow Your Accountancy Practice* (see Figure 6.8).

When we launched into the small business sector I wrote *The FORMULA* (see Figure 6.9).

Figure 6.8:

*The book we used to launch
our sales and marketing
network for accountants*

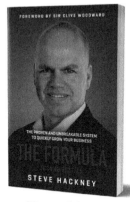

Figure 6.9:

*The book we used to launch
our mentoring programme
into the small business sector*

Figure 6.10:

*The book we used to launch
our community of mentors,
coaches and consultants*

When we launched into the mentoring, coaching and consulting industry to create our community of mentors, I wrote *Business Mentoring Success* (see Figure 6.10).

When we launched into the established service business market, I wrote this book.

Your goal is not to become a celebrated author making money from the sales of your book. You'll use your book to become a celebrated expert specifically with your Perfect Clients, so you significantly increase sales, and you acquire as many clients as you can handle!

Does that make sense?

The book is simply a heavyweight champion in helping you generate leads and clients from your carefully selected group of Perfect Clients.

... and because of that, you can bypass all the normal routes for getting your book published, which means you can often start, finish and print your book within two months.

Yes JUST TWO MONTHS.

So, although there's no harm at all in trying to secure a book publisher, it really isn't necessary. Remember, you're not looking to be a celebrated author making 10% from each book sale. You can self-publish and potentially make thousands even from one book that's in the hands of a Perfect Client.

Don't let your ego get in the way of this.

Even without a publisher, your book is as real and as important as if you'd used a publisher, and it doesn't prevent you from selling it in all major bookstores and, of course, on Amazon and other online book retailers.

So, save your time and self-publish, it's so much easier and will save you months and months.

What follows then is the process I've used to write my last three books (*The FORMULA*, *Business Mentoring Success* and this book). It's also the same process I advise my clients to follow.

Now, even though you're short-cutting the whole book publishing process, you're still going to produce an amazing book. I'm just giving you a simple blueprint to follow to get your book completed in quick time.

Here's the process ...

Step #1: Commit to a Writing Schedule

This is THE most important step. As you are probably aware, it takes most people months and months, often years, to write a book. In the main that's because they don't commit to a daily regimen of writing.

But if all you do is commit yourself to a daily routine of writing for a specific period of time, I can assure you, your book will be written in a matter of weeks, NOT months or years.

Typically, a business book will have between 250 and 350 pages. So, let's say, on average, it's 300 pages. Remember, these are not A4 pages but typically A5 pages (half the size), so it's not as daunting as you may think.

You then decide how long you want it to take to write 300 pages (bear with me). Because I'm experienced in this process, my target, depending on my work schedule, is to write 20 pages a day. That's the commitment I make to myself and my book.

That means it will take me just 15 days to write a 300-page book (all things being equal).

But I may commit to only ten pages a day, which in that case would take me 30 days to write the book.

With this approach, you basically aim to write the target number of pages each day and you don't stop writing until you achieve that.

Alternatively, you agree how much time per day you're willing to commit to writing and accept that some days you'll write more pages than others.

I've used both approaches, and they each work very well.

Remember, you're already an expert in the services you provide. You have an enormous amount of knowledge already in your head, and maybe in blog posts and other things you've written before.

I promise, you'll be surprised how easy it is for you to write a 300-page book.

The spreadsheet shown in Figure 6.11 is the exact schedule for writing the first edition of *The FORMULA*. I promise you, this is what it took, to the minute, to write the book. In this example, I committed myself to writing 20 pages a day (or as close to that as time would allow). There were a couple of days where things didn't quite go to plan (18 August: the day after a night out!), but on the whole you can see I stuck to my writing routine, and it took only 15 days to write the entire book.

I had written a number of blogs and articles, which I used for some sections of the book, and that obviously helped cut down the time, but most chapters I had to write from scratch.

The FORMULA Book - Progress Chart

DATE	START	FINISH	TIME TAKEN	PAGES COMPLETED	CUMULATIVE PAGES	PROJECTED PAGES
10-Aug	9.30	1.20	3 hrs 50 mins	20	20	20
11-Aug	8.21	11.39	3 hrs 20 mins	20	40	40
12-Aug	6.30	10.00	3 hrs 30 mins	24	64	60
13-Aug	6.05	9.15	3 hrs 10 mins	28	92	80
14-Aug	5.50	8.00	2 hrs 10 mins	21	113	100
15-Aug	5.45	8.30	2 hrs 45 mins	21	134	120
16-Aug	5.30	8.10	2 hrs 40 mins	30	164	140
17-Aug	5.40	8.40	3 hrs 0 mins	20	184	160
18-Aug	5.45	6.45	1 hr 0 mins	5	189	180
19-Aug	6.20	7.40	1 hr 20 mins	20	209	200
20-Aug	6.35	11.25	4 hrs 50 mins	25	234	220
21-Aug	6.05	9.25	3 hrs 20 mins	19	253	240
22-Aug	5.35	8.40	3 hrs 5 mins	23	276	260
23-Aug	6.00	9.30	3 hrs 30 mins	20	296	280
24-Aug	5.30	12.00	6 hrs 30 mins	editing	299	300
24-Aug	12.00	12.15	0 hrs 15 mins	to proofreader		
31-Aug	Book to printers					
06-Sep	Proof done					
27-Sep	Book delivered					

Figure 6.11. My Progress Chart for Writing The FORMULA

I start every weekday at 4.55 a.m., so as you can see, I get most of my writing done early in the morning. This also ensures there are no interruptions and, to be frank, it makes it so much easier to write before the day starts.

The FORMULA took 15 days to write ... and then another day for me to edit the book before sending it to the proof-reader/editor.

On average, I dedicated three hours per day, which worked for me at that time.

If you can dedicate, say, two hours only, then that's of course fine, but I wouldn't commit to anything less than two hours per day. You get huge 'economies of scale' the longer you write. In other words, each time you write, you'll start slowly, then pick up pace and keep accelerating until you stop. And two hours is a good sweet spot to take advantage of the speed you gain as you progress.

I also recommend you try and commit to a daily routine. Again, you'll benefit from economies of scale, because your brain will remember more about the writing process, and it will take you less time to get back 'in the groove' so to speak.

If it takes you two hours to write ten pages, then a 300-page book will take you just 30 days. WOW!

That's the power of having a writing schedule.

Step #2: Use a Good Proof-Reader/Editor

I've yet to read an entire book without spotting at least one small typo (my books are no different!). So, no matter how good your proof-reader or editor is, it's rare that you will have a 100% flawless book. But it is very important you do minimise grammatical errors and typos. There's nothing worse than a book with a litany of mistakes, and it's unnecessary.

I don't recommend you proof-read yourself, even if you're good at it, because your brain just won't see the errors, because you've written it. So, spend a few hundred pounds, dollars or euros, and source a good proof-reader.

If you don't already work with one, the best place to find this kind of talent is to use Upwork (www.upwork.com). Simply place your job specification (proof-reading and editing of my 300 page book), and you'll have a number of proposals within 48 hours from experienced and professional proof-readers and book editors.

Make sure you read their reviews and then choose the person that you think would be best suited to working with you.

Step #3: Get a Designer to Create the Cover

You want the book to look great, so I advise you use a designer to create the book cover for you. That includes the front and back covers and the spine.

Figure 6.12 shows the cover for *Business Mentoring Success*. Notice the three sections (front cover, spine and back cover) are created as a single page. This is how the book printer will want you to format it.

In terms of the front cover itself, I strongly recommend you use a good-quality profile picture of yourself. Make sure you're smiling, and dressed in a way that it appropriate for the services you're selling and who your Perfect Clients are. You know this instinctively, but don't change this 'look and feel' for the book.

Using your own photo is important. People will connect with you more, and even if you don't personally meet clients, it still shows the human element of the business and reinforces your expertise.

And don't worry about you being 'the face' of the company. Yes, as you know, clients have a desire to want to work with the main person or people in the business (usually the owners), and you may suffer from this now, but in Chapter 8, I'll explain how you overcome this.

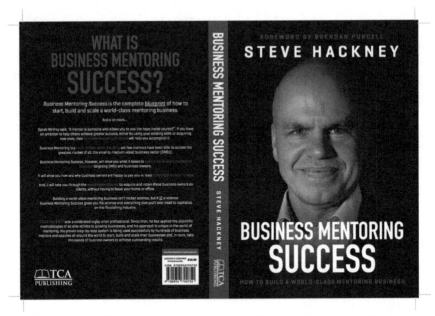

Figure 6.12. The Artwork for the Cover of Business Mentoring Success

Just trust me on this ... using your own profile picture on the front cover is by far the best approach.

Step #4: Get an ISBN

Even though you're self-publishing, you're still going to create a commercially available book. To do this you need to get an ISBN for your book.

An ISBN is an international book number and is unique to your book. You can purchase it from a number of sources. If you're in the UK, I recommend purchasing and registering your ISBN from Nielsen Book:

https://nielsenbook.co.uk/

Step #5: Source a Book Printer

You may be surprised to know that the self-publishing industry is huge. The global print market is said to be worth around $50 billion and growing year on year, and, according to Report Buyer's book printing report, self-publishing is the fastest-growing segment.

You're not entering a small, antiquated market when you self-publish but a well-established, multi-billion industry that's seeing big year-on-year leaps in growth.

Therefore, finding a book printer isn't difficult. Simply type 'book printer' into Google, and you'll get a number of printers to choose from!

Typically, from receiving your book and then agreeing the proof, it will take no more than 3–4 weeks before you're in receipt of your own stunning book! And let me tell you, it's a fantastic feeling.

Crowd Pulling Synergy

Now, you know the three best Crowd Pullers to use, and if you use just one, you'll get great results.

But there is a way to get multiplied results.

I liken this to organising a music festival.

Organisers of the top festivals know that the band line up is crucial to getting a sell-out. They know that if they just have just one headline act, they are severely limiting their market, and therefore potential numbers drop. However, with multiple headline acts that other audiences are fans of, they know that they are reaching a wider market, and that their chances of a sell-out are significantly improved.

And it's just like your own Crowd Pullers.

People like consuming different types of media and formats.

Some like reading reports, because they're short in time consumption. Others (like myself) love reading books, even though it takes several hours. And others enjoy attending webinars, because they can consume a lot of information even in an hour.

And there is still a big percentage of people who will enjoy consuming two or all three formats.

So, to get the best possible results (and I'll talk more about this later in Chapter 9: Putting Your Growth on Autopilot) you should have ALL THREE Crowd Pullers in place.

Start with your Special Report, then write and publish your book, then create your webinar or on-demand training.

Obviously, you'll do this over a period of several months, but if you start with the end in mind, knowing you will have all three Crowd Pullers in place, then I promise you they will be a significant factor in the growth and scaling of your service business.

Getting Your Crowd Puller into the Hands of Your Perfect Clients

Once you create your first Crowd Puller you then, of course, need to get it into the hands of your Perfect Clients. I'll explain exactly how you do that in Step 4 of the Lead Generation System. But first, now you've created your Crowd Puller, you need to create your Lead Capture Page ...

Step #2: LEAD CAPTURE PAGE

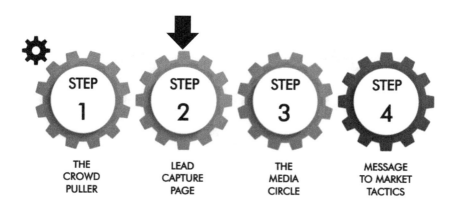

This is another area where most service businesses falter. More often than not they send traffic and visitors to the home page of their website or to a poorly constructed landing page, and then they go straight for the sale.

However, as you're discovering, you need a strategic system that turns your visitor (Perfect Client) into a lead and then into a client, customer or patient, and then into a long-term advocate.

It all starts with the lead.

And you'll use a Lead Capture Page to convert the visitor into a lead.

Figuratively speaking, you need the visitor to hold up their hand and say, 'Yes I'm interested; here are my details'. That's the primary objective of the Lead Capture Page.

The good news is that having identified your Perfect Clients and created your Crowd Puller, your Lead Capture Page virtually writes itself.

As you can see from Figure 6.13, to get the best possible results, in other words, maximising the number of visitors who convert into a lead, there are seven elements that you must include in any and all of your Lead Capture Pages ...

1. A powerful pre-headline that calls out your Perfect Clients.

2. An attention-grabbing headline.

3. Benefit-laden bullet points or sentences.

4. An opt-in form.

5. An opt-in button.

6. A hero shot.

7. A logo.

Let's expand on each one in turn ...

Pre-Headline

The purpose of your pre-headline is to call out to your Perfect Clients. When a Perfect Client lands on your page, they must immediately know that 'this is for them'.

Your pre-headline simply states who they are.

For example ...

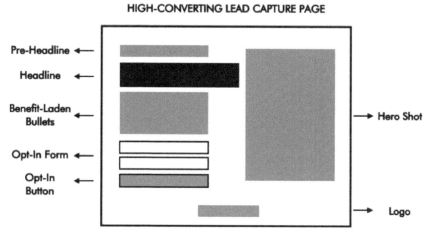

Figure 6.13. The Anatomy of a High-Converting Opt-In Page

- for established service businesses

- for high-net-worth people

- for busy mums over 40

- for ambitious accountants

- for property investors

- for event businesses

- for business coaches, mentors and consultants

Instead of using the word *for* at the start of your pre-head, you can replace that with the word *attention'*. This also works very well.

Do you see how easy this is?

You can see you're already using the power of your Perfect Client Avatar Profile!

Headline

The purpose of your headline is to grab the attention of your visitor.

Without question, it is THE most important part of your page.

As long as you've followed my advice already and created a scintillating title for your Special Report, webinar/on-demand training and your book, the headline is simply a copy of that.

So, if the title of your Special Report is '7 Security Secrets Used by Royalty and Heads of State to Create an "Iron Fortress" Around Their Family, Their Assets and Businesses', then you simply use that as your headline.

Bullet Points

Just because your Crowd Puller is free, it doesn't mean you don't have to work hard to 'sell' it to your Perfect Clients.

That's why we created a compelling attention-grabbing headline for it, and that's why you need to use bullet points to bring out the key reasons why someone should opt-in and receive it.

Do not underestimate the importance of your bullets.

If the headline doesn't quite do the job, your bullets should compel people to opt-in.

The good news is that you can create powerful bullet points using the following bullet templates ...

- How to ...

- Quick and easy ...

- Five simple ways to ...

- No more ...

- The vital ingredients ...

- Discover ...

- Introducing ...

- The secret of ...

- The no-lose way to ...

- 4 facts you must know about ...

- A simple technique for ...

- How to quickly and easily ...

- New ways to ...

Use 3–6 bullets to convey the benefits of your Crowd Puller.

Opt-In Form

My recommendation here is for you to request only two or three pieces of information from your Perfect Prospects; their first name, their email address and, potentially, their mobile phone number.

Remember, the objective of your Lead Capture Page is exactly that ... to get the details of your Perfect Clients so they become a lead. Once you have their details, you can then nurture them by email and SMS.

The rule is simple: the more information you request, the lower your conversion will be from visitor to opt-in.

With your Special Report, 90% of the time you'll need only their first name and email address. With a webinar, getting their mobile as well is useful, because you can remind them by email and SMS prior to the webinar starting.

Of course, when they request your book, you'll be getting their full details, including their mailing address.

Opt-In Button

Your opt-in button is very important. When a Perfect Client enters their details and then presses the button, you are involving them in the sales process. They are taking action, and this is a powerful psychological part of selling. Pressing the button also achieves two other things ...

1. It forwards your Perfect Client to the start of your Conversion System (which, irrespective of the Crowd Puller you're using, will be your Expertise Reinforcement Offer Page, as discussed in the next chapter).

2. It 'pushes' the data to your email and SMS automation system (also discussed in the next chapter) so you can nurture your Perfect Clients, strategically guiding them through your Conversion System.

It is also crucial that your button is placed above the 'fold'. This means that once your Lead Capture Page loads, the button can be seen on the screen without scrolling down. Just trust me on this. We've conducted numerous tests (and every aspect of the perfect Lead Capture Page), and if your button loads below the fold, your opt-ins will tail off alarmingly.

Hero Shot

Your hero shot is simply the image of your Special Report or book. If your Crowd Puller is a webinar/on-demand training, then the hero shot should be a smiling profile picture of yourself.

Once again, don't underestimate the importance of your hero shot. It should be a high-resolution image that's crisp and looks stunning to the eye.

The combination of the pre-head, headline, bullets and hero shot will ensure you create a high-converting Lead Capture Page, so simply follow my advice here to ensure you convert a high percentage of Perfect Clients into leads.

Logo

I know, I know ... you've agonised over your branding. You've probably spent several hundred pounds or even thousands on your logo (one of our clients paid £12,000 for theirs – prior to working with us I hasten to add!). You're proud of how your branding and logo looks, and you want to show it upfront and central, right?

Now, before I tell you a potentially uncomfortable home truth about your brand and your logo, let me preface it with the fact that I do believe your branding and logo ARE important. It's how you use them that is the BIG difference.

You see, unless your brand is a household name, such as Coke, McDonalds or Apple, then your brand stands for nothing in the eyes of your Perfect Clients.

Read that last sentence again (it's crucial you 'get' this).

When you're a household name, your brand has immense value.

The downside is that getting to this level of recognition costs hundreds of millions, and I'm pretty sure you don't have that kind of money slewing around in your business right now. Correct?

All your Perfect Clients care about is this ...

'What's in it for me?'

In other words, what do you provide that's going to improve my life or my business?

What problem or problems does your service solve?

Why should I choose you over your competition ... and so on.

That has absolutely NOTHING to do with your branding or your logo.

However, as I said, your branding and logo are important, because we want your business to look good in terms of its branding and logo.

But you build your brand ultimately by selling MORE of your services, not by focusing your marketing and advertising on it!

Do you see the difference?

That's why your logo should be placed at the BOTTOM of your Lead Capture Page and reduced in size so it isn't overwhelming.

Look at it this way ...

You will get eyeballs on your branding and logo. Every person who lands on your page will see it, but it's a by-product of doing things correctly, NOT of putting your branding upfront and in their faces!

Don't sulk.

This may seem trivial to you, or it may be a huge thing (depending on how invested you are about your branding), but trust me, if you focus on your brand and make it the central piece in your marketing and advertising (like so many service businesses wrongly do), then you are, figuratively speaking, putting a plug in your sales funnel, and fewer people will convert into clients, customers or patients.

I've warned you!

Okay, so now you have a stunning Lead Capture Page that's optimised to generate leads from your Perfect Clients.

Let's now move on to how we get them to your Lead Capture Page ...

Step #3: THE MEDIA CIRCLE

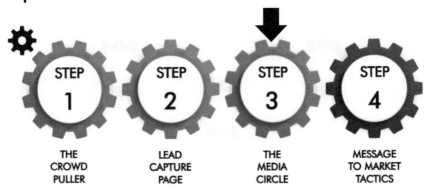

As I mentioned earlier, I started Hackney Marketing Consultants way back in the mid-1990s.

Back then, as I've already mentioned, the internet had only just started. So, to generate leads I was reliant on traditional routes to market, such as direct mail and advertising in publications.

If you're old enough to remember what it was like 'pre-internet' you'll recall that direct mail – in other words, sending letters, postcards, leaflets, invitations, and so on through conventional mail that would be delivered by the good old postman – was at its height in terms of popularity.

It was kind of like how email is today. Other than on a Sunday, we'd all get dozens of items through the post at home and at work, which meant you'd have to work REALLY hard to grab attention, so that your piece didn't end up in the bin before even being opened!

Advertising in publications, on radio and on television were the other main routes to market, but they were all expensive, even to get started. Remember, there was no digital television or digital radio back then either, so there were only a few TV and radio channels compared to hundreds today.

All the media companies basically had a monopoly on the routes to market, and therefore you had to pay through the nose to start any campaign.

Direct mail was therefore the cheapest and least risky.

It was still a big gamble, because you had to spend your hard-earned money first *before* launching any campaign.

But now we're so lucky.

We are blessed with having almost limitless routes to market.

You've still got the traditional channels, as above, and you've also got everything online from email through to social media marketing and advertising on huge platforms such as Google, YouTube, Facebook, Twitter, Instagram, and so on. Believe me, it's never been better or easier!

And as long as you've created your Perfect Client Avatar Profile, you'll have a good idea of how you can reach those Perfect Clients.

In this context, the *how* means the channels you will use to send your tailored message to your Perfect Clients.

However, because there's a proliferation of routes to market, it has become harder to choose the *right* channels.

So, I'm going to explain what your options are and how you can best approach generating leads.

To start with, most service businesses I come across use only one main method to generate leads, which is a dangerous approach.

It's dangerous because if you use just one tactic, and for some reason it stops working, you've got a big problem on your hands. Instead, you must use a variety of lead generation channels and tactics, and providing you follow the advice in this book, you'll multiply the results you get and make it so much easier to scale your service business.

I'm about to reveal an approach that very few people outside our inner circle of clients use.

I promise, it is the best way for you to determine which lead generation channels and tactics you should use for YOUR service business to reach YOUR Perfect Clients.

More importantly, it maximises your results, because you're not reliant on one channel or tactic. In this context, when I talk about 'channels', I am referring to the way in which your lead generation tactic is delivered to your Perfect Clients.

As I mentioned above, most people become reliant on one channel and one tactic, and you only have to look at how difficult Facebook has made things over the years in terms of banning ads and even banning whole accounts. In fact, only a few months before writing this chapter, Facebook's entire platform went down for six hours.

I cannot stress enough that if you're solely reliant on just one channel and one tactic, it WILL end in tears at some point.

Dan Kennedy, the great direct marketing guru in the USA, said, 'The worst number in business is one'. I agree. One main supplier. One record-breaking salesperson. One route to market!

It's been my experience that many service business owners leave small fortunes on the table, simply because they've failed to *choose* the correct channels and tactics to reach their Perfect Clients.

The good news is that you're already way ahead of your competitors, because you've identified your Perfect Clients, and you know where to find them and where they hang out, which means you can strategically select the most appropriate channels to reach them.

And once you've chosen your channels, the lead generation tactics then select themselves.

This is a very simple yet highly effective way to determine the right channels to use for your service business.

First, let's look at the channels available to you. I call them 'Media Channels'.

These days, most people think there is really only one Media Channel: the internet! But there are, in fact, three Media Channels available to you …

1. **E-Media** – everything online.

2. **P-Media** – everything that's published and printed.

3. **DM-Media** – everything sent in the post or delivered through a letterbox using direct mail.

And to optimise your results and scale your business (see more in Chapter 11: Scaling Up Part 1: Pump THE MACHINE with Channels and Tactics), you'll want to ideally use all three channels to reach your Perfect Clients, but at the very least two and a variety of tactics within each one.

I call this approach the 'Media Circle', as shown in Figure 6.14.

If you see your routes to market as a complete circle, to maximise results you need to use all three channels, otherwise the circle isn't whole.

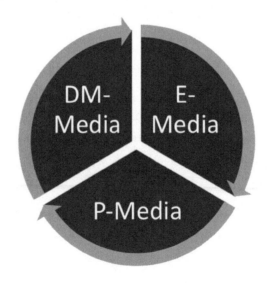

Figure 6.14. The Media Circle

This vividly shows why you shouldn't use a marketing agency or digital marketing agency, or simply someone who has expertise in, say, just Facebook advertising, or just Google Ads or just on direct mail or just in offline advertising ... and so on.

Ideally, you need expertise across all three Media Channels. Otherwise, you won't be capitalising on *ALL THREE* channels to reach your Perfect Clients.

Figure 6.15 shows the three Media Channels and some of the corresponding tactics you can use to reach your Perfect Clients.

Obviously, the list is endless. However, I'll explain exactly how you choose the right tactics shortly, and it's much easier than you may think ...

MEDIA CHANNEL	TACTICS
1. E-Media	• website/landing pages • webinars • email marketing • Google and Google Ads • YouTube advertising • YouTube channels • Facebook and Facebook advertising • LinkedIn and LinkedIn advertising •

	<ul><li>Twitter and Twitter advertising</li><li>other social media platforms such as Instagram, Pinterest, etc.</li><li>other search engines</li><li>online press releases</li><li>online publishing</li><li>... etc.</li></ul>

2. P-Media	<ul><li>classified advertising</li><li>newspaper, magazine and trade press advertising</li><li>business directories advertising</li><li>inserts</li><li>radio advertising</li><li>TV Advertising</li><li>press releases</li><li>... etc.</li></ul>

3. DM-Media	<ul><li>seminars</li><li>letters</li><li>postcards</li><li>flyers</li></ul>

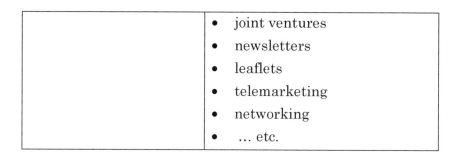

	• joint ventures • newsletters • leaflets • telemarketing • networking • ... etc.

Figure 6.15. Media Channels and Tactics

So, how do you choose the right Media Channels and tactics for your service business?

All you need to do is ask yourself the following two simple questions:

1. Where can my Perfect Clients be reached?

2. Where would my Perfect Clients look to source our services?

The answers to these two questions will help you to determine which marketing channels and tactics to use, and they are shown in Figure 6.16.

But remember, as I mentioned earlier, I recommend you use all three or a minimum of two Media Channels to reach your Perfect Clients. Thousands of tests have proven that if you use a combination of two or, ideally, three categories, your results massively improve.

CHOOSING THE RIGHT CHANNELS AND TACTICS		
Where can the target market be found?	**Media Channel**	**Tactics**
At work or in their business	DM-Media	• letters • postcards • flyers • invitations • seminars • joint ventures • newsletters • leaflets • telemarketing

At home	DM-Media	• letters • postcards • flyers • invitations • seminars • joint ventures • newsletters • leaflets • telemarketing

Subscribing to trade press	P-Media	• classified advertising • trade press advertising • inserts • press releases

Internet	E-Media	• website/Landing Pages • webinars • email marketing • Google and Google Ads • YouTube advertising • YouTube channels • Facebook and Facebook advertising • LinkedIn and LinkedIn Advertising

Internet (cont'd)	E-Media	• Twitter and Twitter advertising • other social media platforms such as Instagram, Pinterest, etc. • online publishers • other search engines • online press releases

Local newspaper	P-Media	• classified ads • newspaper ads • inserts • press releases

Figure 6.16. Choosing the Right Channels and Tactics

As you can see, you have numerous options in terms of the tactics to use within each Media Channel.

But remember, it all starts from your Perfect Clients and the two questions you ask to determine the best channels and tactics to use.

My advice is to first choose what you think is the best channel and the best tactic within that channel, and then once you're getting good results (I'll explain exactly what that means shortly), then add another tactic within that same channel or move on to the next channel and so on.

This is one of the key *Scaling Parameters* which I cover with you in Chapter 11.

But before moving on to Step 4 of the Lead Generation System, I want to explain how you can use your Perfect Client Avatar Profile in each Media Channel to ensure you're targeting only your Perfect Clients.

Listen up, because this is one of the most insightful and important lessons in this entire book, and if you get this right (when you get it right!), it will literally transform your results ...

The Advanced Precision Targeting Model

As I mentioned earlier, your Perfect Client Avatar Profile is the tool you'll use to ensure you're targeting the right people or businesses.

I'm now going to show you how you're going to use your Avatar Profile to devastating effect across all three Media Channels.

Let me introduce you to my 'Advanced Precision Targeting Model', as shown in Figure 6.17) ...

THE MACHINE

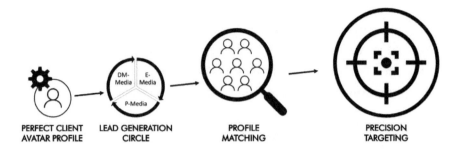

| PERFECT CLIENT
AVATAR PROFILE | LEAD GENERATION
CIRCLE | PROFILE
MATCHING | PRECISION
TARGETING |

Figure 6.17. Precision Targeting Model

Perfect Client Avatar Profile

You've already created your Avatar Profile.

Lead Generation Circle

You now know there are three Media Channels (E, DM and P) you can use to reach your Perfect Client Avatar Profile.

Profile Matching

For each Media Channel, you're now going to use their relevant profile matching tools. In other words, you're going to match the profile of your Perfect Clients so you're targeting only the exact Avatar Profile you've identified within each media Channel.

This is the key step.

You see, irrespective of the Media Channel you're using, you'll be able to almost perfectly match your Perfect Clients so that when you launch your tactics, they are being directed ONLY to your Perfect Clients.

Let me explain how you do this ...

Lead Generation System

Let's start with E-Media. To keep things simple, let's say your Avatar Profile is event businesses in the UK with a turnover of £500,000 to £10 million, and you're targeting the business owners to help them run and manage their businesses more profitably.

You decide to create an email campaign to reach your Perfect Clients. So, you choose your email provider, and they have a 'data specification', which lists the different parameters you can choose to target the right people.

You send them your Avatar Profile, and then they match your profile with their data specification, and they tell you there are 4890 businesses on their email list that fit your profile! Perfect!

You also decide to run a LinkedIn InMail campaign. You log in to your LinkedIn advertising account, and you once again use their targeting profile to identify your Perfect Clients. LinkedIn doesn't have turnover bandings, but they do have 'number of employees', so you make a calculated decision (because you know your market) and decide to select event companies with 26–200 employees (you select 11–25, 26–50 and 51–200).

You also decide to run a YouTube In-Stream Video campaign. You initially decide to run a 'keyword-based' campaign (there are many others), so, again using your knowledge of the industry, you select 50+ keywords that Google (YouTube is owned by Google) have identified as being right for your business. Keywords include 'how to grow my event business', 'growing my event business', and so on.

Next, let's turn to P-Media ...

You then research the publishing industry and find publications that are perfectly focused on your Avatar Profile. *Event Magazine* and *Event Marketer* both provide a breakdown of the readership, and although a percentage of the readers are running small events businesses, many of the business types you're targeting also subscribe to both magazines.

And finally, you look at DM-Media.

You look online for a mailing list provider. You find one that has a good reputation, and you send them your Avatar Profile to match against their database of businesses. They come back to you with a perfect matching list of 3620 businesses.

This is not theory; this is a real-life scenario for one of our clients.

This is the level of targeting that's now available to you.

'But Steve, I'm not running a business-to-business service company; I'm running a business-to-consumer one'.

It doesn't matter.

You can use the same process I've just taken you through, and in many respects the profile matching is even better.

For example, if I take DM-Media, you can target a huge number of profiling criteria with absolute precision. For instance, here's just a small selection of profiling selections you can make when targeting Perfect Clients ...

- age

- household income

- property value

- property type

- year property built

- length of residency

- tenure status

- children age range

- number of children

- number of adults

- household affluence

- household composition (number of bedrooms, etc.)

- mortgage value or no mortgage

- directorship

- shareholding

- publications subscribed to

- and so on!

Precision Targeting

As you can see, when you define your Perfect Client Avatar Profile, select your Media Channels, then use 'Profile Matching' you're moving away from scattergun or mass-market targeting and moving into the little-used but highly powerful and profitable world of Precision Targeting.

The approaches are miles apart, and the moment you adopt this approach, your business is going to fly!

Having decided on the channel and the tactic you're going to use, your next step is to create your 'Message to Market Tactics' ...

Step #4: MESSAGE TO MARKET TACTICS

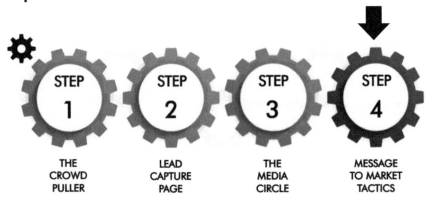

Of course, this will take many different forms depending on the tactic being used, and as new online platforms spring up different tactics will come into play (innovation is really occurring only in the E-Media channel).

But I want to give you a system for creating your tactics that works with ALL of them and will work with any new tactics that are developed over the coming years, irrespective of which of the three Media Channels it is in. In other words, this is an 'evergreen' approach that will keep working and working for you.

Of course, each tactic has its own nuances (explained shortly), but what I'm about to give you is arguably the most successful approach to tactic creation ever devised, and you're going to love it.

Over the years, this one approach has helped to generate millions of leads and hundreds and hundreds of millions in sales.

As I said, it works across all Media Channels and all tactics. But you can do it effectively only once you've created your Perfect Client Avatar Profile.

You have to have a good understanding of who your Perfect Clients are, because as you're going to see, in EVERY tactic you create you're going to MATCH THE MESSAGE TO THE MARKET. Yes, every tactic you create from this day forward will have a message that reaches out to your Perfect Clients, compelling them to take action.

And to do this you're going to use something I call the 'Core Elements'. I wrote about them in detail in both my previous books (*The FORMULA* and *Business Mentoring Success*), but I'm going to go deeper here, because they will put the lead generation of your service business on a completely new level.

Let me be clear: this is a system and approach that you use FOR ALL YOUR TACTICS ... existing tactics, new tactics and future ones that aren't even in existence right now. This is an approach for the ages. And I promise that when you apply it, your results are going to multiply literally overnight.

When I'm working with our clients, one of the first things we do is apply the Core Elements across all their existing tactics.

As you're going to see, they are missing from almost every tactic you're currently using, or if they are being used, they are being implemented poorly. Therefore, with ZERO extra spend, by applying the Core Elements we can instantly ramp up results, and often multiply results. That's the power of the Core Elements.

So, I'm going to take your through the Core Elements and also give you something that I've never shared before other than with my team and our army of 'Business Growth Mentors' that will give you a truly amazing way to score the effectiveness of your tactic BEFORE you even launch it. I'll give it to you in Chapter 12 when I'm discussing Marginal Gains with you. Nothing like this exists anywhere in the world, but I wanted you to have it, because it's such a staggering way to optimise every tactic you create now and in the future.

My team and I use this exact same approach before launching any tactic for our business or for our clients' businesses

What I'm going to do now is take you through each of the nine Core Elements (see diagram shown in Figure 6.18). I'll explain exactly what each one is, give you its 'success formula', and present good and bad examples so you can gain a greater understanding of them, making it easier to apply to your own service business.

I can tell you that this level of deep understanding can be gained only after years and years of study, testing and application. However, I'm going to give you all this on a plate so you can use it immediately in your service business to great effect. I promise that once you've finished this section, you'll be armed with the nine most powerful tools on this planet to create powerful, profitable and highly engaging tactics, and you'll be able to use them to achieve anything and everything you ever dreamed of.

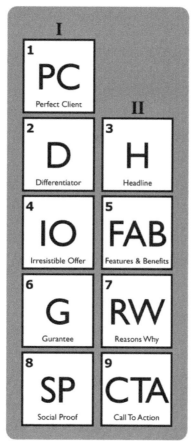

Figure 6.18. The Nine Core Elements

I don't believe any of the nine Core Elements are necessarily new to you. For example, I'm pretty sure you've heard of 'features and benefits', but I can guarantee you won't be using most of the Core Elements, and that those you do use won't be applied correctly or used to maximum effect. And right now, you have no way of knowing what 'good' looks like and how you can transform them so they optimise your results.

And remember, just to reiterate, all nine Core Elements are FREE to use. They don't cost a penny to apply to your tactics, yet they have the POWER to *multiply your results.*

So, even if you're using a tactic that's currently working, when you apply the Core Elements to it or transform the Core Elements already in your specific tactic, you'll see significant and often exponential gains.

But before I take you through them, there's one thing you must do before creating your tactic, and that is to do something virtually no one does ...

Set Your Primary Objective for Each Tactic

People get this so, so wrong. In fact, most people don't even do it. But think about it ...

If you don't know what your primary objective is for your tactic how can you create it? Yes, you already know one thing, it must be tailored to your Target Market Avatar Profile, but that's not the primary objective.

The primary objective is simply this ...

What is the ACTION
you want your Perfect Client to take?

Write that down and stick it on your desk.

This is one of the biggest mistakes I see across the entire marketing and advertising spectrum.

Now, I'm taking you through a specific set system on how to generate leads. I'll then take you through a set and specific system for you to use to convert those leads into sales. I'll then take you through a set and specific system to maximise the value and profitability of every client.

It's a 'nurturing' system with a number of strategic steps built in, designed to take a 'stranger' and convert them into a high-profit Perfect Client.

I am NOT advocating an approach where you try and take a stranger and in one step try to convert them into a high-profit Perfect Client. That's akin to walking up to a complete stranger in a bar and asking them to marry you.

Clearly, unless you're Brad Pitt or Angelina Jolie, the odds are stacked heavily against you, but if you first introduce yourself, ask if they would like a drink and then take time to get to know them, date them, and so on, then clearly your chances of ultimately marrying them are significantly increased.

It's no different when selling your services.

And this is key to your success ...

The objective of your tactic is simply to get the Perfect Client to move to the NEXT step in your system.

Not the next three steps, not the next two steps, but the NEXT step.

Let me put this into context ...

I'm taking you through the steps you need to take to get your Lead Generation System in place.

But in terms of the 'journey' you're taking your Perfect Clients on, it looks like the path shown in Figure 6.19 ...

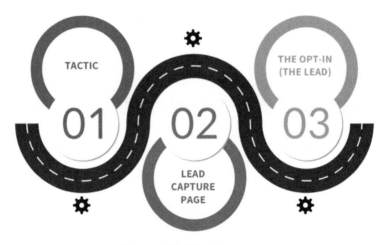

Figure 6.19. The Journey

And to determine the primary objective, it's simply the next stage in the journey. Therefore, the primary objective of your *tactic* is to simply get your Perfect Client to your *Lead Capture Page*, not to get the opt-in or get them to buy from you. Do you follow?

So, what's the primary objective of the *Lead Capture Page*?

That's right, to get the Opt-In, and so on.

I promise you, this is absolutely critical for you to understand and apply, and it will make a huge difference to your results, especially when you also create your Message to Market Tactics.

Okay, you're now ready for the Core Elements, so let's dig in ...

Core Element #1: PERFECT CLIENTS

As you know, I have already dedicated a whole chapter to identifying your Perfect Clients and creating your Perfect Client Avatar Profile.

The success of THE MACHINE depends on it, because you're tailoring every part of it to them.

And when it comes to your Lead Generation System and creating Message to Market Tactics, it's no different.

This is the essence and the 'secret sauce' to creating incredibly successful tactics.

The rule is simple: EVERY tactic you create MUST be completely focused on your Perfect Clients. You're going to match the message (the content in every tactic) to your Perfect Clients.

And ALL of the other eight Core Elements which follow will be tailored to your Perfect Clients to ensure your entire message in every tactic is laser-beam focused on your Perfect Clients.

Got it?

I've trained literally thousands of people on this, but many of them don't truly 'get it'. You must move away from general poorly targeted tactics to precision-based targeting that reach out to your Perfect Clients like a heat-seeking missile. The ONLY way to do that effectively is to tailor absolutely everything to them.

Core Element #2: DIFFERENTIATOR

A differentiator is the one thing that sets you apart from the competition. It's WHY your Perfect Clients should choose you over and above anyone else. Communicating this uniqueness is a powerful and persuasive part of each tactic you create.

This is a very weak area for almost every service business and one which really hinders growth.

THAT'S WHY I DEDICATED AN ENTIRE CHAPTER TO 'PRODUCTISING YOUR SERVICES'.

Doing that gives you something that differentiates you from the competition, and you've done it, remember, without cost.

The problem is that clients, customers and patients have become more discerning, which means they're looking for reasons to change or simply use another business: unique reasons; competitive advantages; things that are desirable to them that no other business can offer them.

But because so few businesses create this uniqueness, most people (rightly or wrongly) think ALL businesses are the same within each industry sector.

So, for example, they think all plumbers are the same, all printers are the same, all lawyers are the same, all event companies are the same, and so on. Changing, for the sake of changing, to another supplier who is just going to be like the existing one just isn't worth the hassle. Better the devil you know!

How can you expect your Perfect Clients to choose your service business over and above any of the competition if they can't quickly see what it is you do which is so unique and so beneficial to them?

And there are other VERY IMPORTANT factors to consider.

If you are viewed by your Perfect Clients as the same as the competition, what do you think becomes the important criterion when they want your service?

That's right: **PRICE.**

There's no hiding the fact that as soon as you create the differentiator for your business, you automatically move away from the 'price war' into the rarefied air of higher prices/fees and less competition! Or – worst case – the same price but the ability to win more business.

You only have to look at what Amazon has done to many product-based businesses who, to all intents and purposes, didn't differentiate themselves. Amazon just copied them, undercut them, leveraged their purchasing power and economies of scale, and won market share. It's put thousands upon thousands of businesses out of business as a consequence.

You must therefore make it as hard as possible for people to compare you with others. That's why Productising Your Services is key to you taking your business to the next level. It rids you of all this nonsense and the potentially business-killing environment many others have suffered over the years.

But I also want you to explore additional areas in your business that could differentiate yourself even more (the more, the better).

As I mentioned earlier, if you can't accurately describe this uniqueness to your prospects, what chance have they got to find out what you offer over and above the competition?

If the prospect can immediately see **what it is you do that is so unique**, and they find it irresistible, you've created the perfect differentiator.

And remember, your differentiator isn't just about being different from the competition; it's about being different from the competition AND providing something of great benefit to your Perfect Clients.

To explain this further, I'm going to give you a scenario I've often used with accountants, who, like most other service providers, are terrible at differentiating their firms. Consequently, most compete on price with 'price slasher' firms.

I pick an accountant in the room and say, 'okay, I'm going to give you a differentiator that I can guarantee no other accounting firm is offering right now. You're going to be called the Pink Accountants. Everything to do with your firm is pink. Your offices are pink. Your stationery is pink. Your website is pink. Your staff wear pink suits, shirts, blouses and dresses.'

Clearly that's a differentiator, but it's of NO benefit to their clients or prospects, so it's useless. Does that make sense?

A differentiator really is one of the most powerful concepts you can apply to your service business, especially, as I said, if you can stack at least one more on top of your service-based 'product' that you created in Chapter 4. The good news is that it can be created relatively quickly and easily using my *differentiator success formula* ...

(U + C + CC) = D

(Uniqueness + Create + Craft and Communicate) = Differentiator

Let's go through it ...

(U) UNIQUENESS

Most service businesses already have a differentiator; they just don't communicate it, because they forget just how important it is.

Your first task is, therefore, to look over your business (including how you service customers, clients or patients), and your services, and identify any differentiator that's already there.

(C) CREATE

Of course, not all businesses have a differentiator. Sometimes you need to create it. There are many ways to do this.

Here are eight proven categories any service business can use to create additional differentiators that you can tailor to your own service business ...

1. New and Unique

Sometimes your service is so new and unique that the service itself is the differentiator, and we've done this already by Productising Your Services.

But is there anything else you can focus on that's unique?

2. Highest Quality

One well-known brand that immediately comes to mind when you think about quality is the international watch leader Rolex. Rolex also has a short differentiator statement that communicates volumes.

```
Rolex - 'Quality Takes Time'
```

3. Expert Status

This type of differentiator is, of course, absolutely perfect when selling services. It communicates the idea that 'I/We am/are the top in my/our field. You can trust my/our knowledge and experience'.

As we discussed earlier, all three Crowd Pullers are the most effective ways of positioning you as an expert.

4. Amazing Customer Service

Providing superior customer service is a wonderful way to add value, as well as develop long-term customer loyalty.

To surpass the competition, you must go beyond simply satisfying customers, you have to AMAZE them.

One of the ways to do this is by using *Moments of Truth* (see Chapter 8), which spotlights every point of contact with your clients, customers or patients, and creates a WOW experience for each one.

5. Speed

The speed at which your service is delivered can be a powerful differentiator. Offering overnight or same-day shipping as your standard service can give you a strong competitive advantage.

For example, FedEx changed the shipping world when they began guaranteeing overnight delivery of packages (obviously a key service required by many people and businesses). Their differentiator has stood the test of time:

```
FedEx - 'When It Absolutely Positively Has to Be
                There Overnight'
```

6. Strongest Guarantee

A powerful guarantee can immediately give you a compelling differentiator. A guarantee is one of the Core Elements and is discussed shortly.

7. Magic Wand

If your Perfect Clients could wave a magic wand over your industry sector, what would they want most?

Some of the greatest businesses in the world were founded on such thinking. For example, Microsoft was built on this premise:

```
'to make the computer accessible
    and easy to use for everyone'
```

In an inexpensive way, can you reposition your basic offer to meet the customers' major need?

8. THE Biggest, Most Important Benefit

This final method is relatively simple. You need to identify every single feature of your product or service, together with how you operate as a business and how you interact with your clients, customers or patients. Then put them in order of importance. The top one could then be a powerful differentiator. Features and Benefits are a Core Element, and I'll be discussing them in detail with you shortly.

A VERY IMPORTANT NOTE ABOUT USING THE LOWEST PRICE AS THE DIFFERENTIATOR

NEVER, EVER DO IT.

Guaranteeing the lowest price has been used as a differentiator for many businesses (the 'slasher firms' I alluded to earlier). However, cutting profit margins too deeply is rarely healthy for a business, even though when running a service business we do generally have the luxury of having sizeable margins to work with. Nevertheless, you want to, at the very least, maintain margins and preferably increase them, and when you follow everything in this book, you'll be able to do that.

Just remember ... there are no prizes for the second cheapest!

(CC) CRAFT AND COMMUNICATE

You should now be left with a fairly short list of options. Now, you need to start crafting your differentiator.

Once you've gone through this stage, if you have two or more options, you'll quickly be able to determine which differentiator really stands out.

Here are the three rules to define your differentiator:

RULE #1: A short differentiator is more powerful than a long one.

RULE #2: Your differentiator should be clear and easy to understand.

RULE #3: Your differentiator should always focus on your Perfect Clients.

Take each of your chosen differentiator categories and write down your differentiator. Make sure you adhere to the three rules above.

Having done this, one differentiator should emerge as a clear front runner.

But you could still have one or more additional ones that are very powerful.

Don't discard them.

You'll use these as well by 'stacking' them on top of each other to create your **'Differentiator Stack'**, which will simply blow your competition out of the water!

You'll then make sure you align your differentiator(s) to your Perfect Clients and then communicate it.

Core Element #3: HEADLINE

Every tactic you use must include a powerful headline. The name of your business, or your logo **is NOT a headline**! This is one of the reasons I told you to place your logo at the bottom of the page when creating your Lead Capture Pages. You don't want it interfering in anyway with your headline!

Headlines are used to grab attention. They should stop your Perfect Clients dead in their tracks.

A poor headline means no matter how good your message, your Perfect Clients will simply pass you by.

Think of it like you're waiting for a bus to stop. You can wait by a proper bus stop (the headline), and 99 times out of 100 the bus will stop and let you on. Or you can take your chances and stand anywhere in the street, hold your hand out and hope the bus will stop. You might get lucky five times in every hundred. That's the difference between a good headline and a bad headline.

And like everything else I'm taking you through in this book, your headline needs to connect with your Perfect Clients. So, using a very simple example to illustrate the point, if your perfect Clients are start-up businesses, then a headline such as ...

`‘Attention Start-Ups: How You Too Can Create a Thriving Business’`

... will attract more attention from your Perfect Clients than a more general headline such as ...

`‘How You Too Can Create A Thriving Business’`

When you see it like this, hopefully you can immediately understand why the headline plays such an important role and why the name of your business really is the worst headline you could ever use!

Think of the headline as the 'ad for the ad'.

If your Perfect Clients dismiss the headline, that's it; you've lost them. They won't engage with whatever tactic you're using and, consequently, they won't take the action you want them to take.

To emphasise the importance of headlines, here are a couple of quotes from two of the most highly respected copywriters of all time.

`'If you can come up with a good headline, you are almost sure to have a good ad. But even the greatest writer can't save an ad with a poor headline.'`

John Caples – *How to Make Your Advertising Make Money*

`'On average, five times as many people read the headline as read the body copy.'`

David Ogilvy – *Confessions of an Advertising Man*

What does this mean? Basically, if you get your headline right, you have a chance. Get it wrong, you have ZERO chance.

The image on the next page highlights a simple example to show how few people understand the basic principle of using headlines.

Although the Yellow Pages printed directory is obviously extinct, it serves as a great example, because it lists all competing businesses on the same page. Look at the image shown in Figure 6.20. It shows the ads in the category 'Cookers, Stoves and Ovens' – 'Repairs and Spares'. This is typical, and if we did it with websites, for example, we'd have similar results.

Typical 'Headlines' That Don't Work!

Figure 6.20. The Lack of Powerful Headlines

Notice the headlines (I've circled them).

Here are the headlines isolated from the ads ...

Repairs Specialists

Kingston Appliances

Electric Ovens and Cookers

We Repair or Replace

A1 Cooker Repairs

CT Appliance Repairs

AH Appliance Services

Four of the 'headlines' are the name of the business, and the other three are meaningless.

NONE of them grabs attention.

And there's the opportunity.

If just one of those businesses had crafted a powerful headline, they'd have won most of the business in an instant!

Just like in this example, because so many people are doing it wrong, if all you do is lead with a strong headline on all your tactics, you'll transform the response and success many times over.

Effective headlines fulfil these four key objectives:

- Get attention.

- Focus on your Perfect Clients.

- Deliver a complete message.

- Draw the reader into the rest of your tactic.

The good news is that creating winning headlines can be achieved by following the *headline success formula ...*

$$(HT + T + F) = H$$

(Headline Template + Test Before Launch + Format) = Headline

(HT) HEADLINE TEMPLATE

As I said, simply adding a powerful headline to all your tactics will multiply your results.

Many of the headline tests we've carried out over the years have resulted in massive increases in results, and that's testing one great headline against the next (not one poor headline against a great headline!).

I've also discovered that there are a number of 'headline templates' which, because of their structure, will always bring results. For example, here's one of my favourites:

HOW TO ...

Simply adding those two words at the start of a headline transforms it into a winner. There are many more. In fact, I've identified over 125 of them.

I've listed seven more of my favourites.

By applying these different headline templates, you'll start to see how you can create winning headlines.

To give you an idea of how easy it is to use these templates, I've created a headline for each template based on one of the 'Cooker and Stove' repair service ads I showed you earlier.

- **Benefit headlines** (All your headlines should contain a benefit of some sort.)

  My Example:

  'Same-Day Repair, or Your Money Back'

- **Use a two- or three-word headline** (but remember long headlines are almost always more successful than short headlines).

  - Get One Month Free

  - Double Bonus Service

  - Oh My God!

  - Gosh!

  - At Last!

  - Millionaire Secrets

  - If Only ...

  My Example:

  'Same-Day Repair'

- **Headlines that focus on quick and easy solutions**

  - Fast and Simple ...

  - Ridiculously Easy and Fast ...

  - Idiot-Proof ...

- In Just Ten Days ...

- The Seven-Minute Workout ...

- The Lazy Man's Way to ...

- Instant, Automatic Results ...

- The Quick and Easy Way to ...

My Example:

`'Your Cooker Repaired Within 24 Hours -`
`Guaranteed'`

- **Warning headlines**

    - Read This Before You ...

    - Don't Choose Another Accountant Until You've Read These Facts

My Example:

`'WARNING: Don't Choose Another Cooker Repair`
`Company Until You've Read This'`

- **Testimonial headlines**

    - A Specific Benefit Written Testimonial from One of Your Customers

    - 'Or It Can Just Be a Headline in Quotation Marks Like This Written Like a Testimonial'

My Example:

`'I Called Them at 9.30 a.m., and My Cooker Was`
`Fixed and Working Like New at 3 p.m. the Same Day`
`- Amazing Service'`

- **Reasons-why headlines**

  - Seven Reasons Why You Should ...

  - 37 Invigorating Reasons ...

  - 6 Ways To ...

  - 7 Steps ...

  - Here's How ...

  My Example:

  '7 Compelling Reasons to Call Us First and Get Your Cooker Repaired the Same Day – Guaranteed'

- **Offer headlines**

  - Put your offer in the headline ...

  - Try-Before-You-Buy Accountancy Service

  My Example:

  'No Call Out Charge and Same-Day Repair, or Your Money Back'

(T) TEST BEFORE LAUNCH

Next, you need to test your headlines.

The ultimate test is, of course, when the tactic goes live, but it's best to do a test prior to launching, because it can save and make you significant sum of money in the process.

To do this you can use the Pre-Launch Headline Test. I discovered this from Dan Kennedy.

Very simply, all you do is isolate the headline and add the words: For more information call us on 0800 123 456.

What you then do is score each headline relative to each other on a scale of 1 to 10, with 10 being perfect.

You'll easily be able to pick one or two winners to go with.

(F) FORMAT

Finally, once you've chosen your headline, you need to format it correctly. That depends on where you're using it, of course. As a basic set of guidelines, your headlines should be set in large type, have quotation marks around them and ideally be no longer than 17 words (of the 100 best headlines ever created, based on resulting sales, only five had more than 17 words).

I've created a Headline Creation Template for you to ensure you never worry again about using an under-performing headline.

You can download it from here:

www.themachine.co.uk/book-resources

Core Element #4: IRRESISTIBLE OFFER

Having an irresistible offer is absolutely essential. The good news is that your 'Crowd Puller' is exactly that and is the irresistible offer you are going to use for your Lead Generation System.

You've created your Crowd Puller to be completely focused on your Perfect Clients, and you've packed it full of value. So, whether it's your Special Report, your webinar/on-demand training or your book, you're good to go, and they will all prove highly irresistible to your Perfect Clients!

Core Element #5: FEATURES AND BENEFITS

Almost every business owner is aware of features and benefits. But it's surprising how few people actually use benefits in their tactics.

All too often, the features are communicated rather than the more powerful corresponding benefits. As a result, the power of your message is reduced significantly.

When you communicate just the features of your service, you're making your Perfect Client do all the work to figure out why they want the feature. It's in your best interest to draw the connection for them. But to do that, you have to know and articulate the results (benefits) yourself.

Benefits are the 'sizzle'; they are the emotional triggers that help in the decision-making process. Elmer Wheeler, the famous sales trainer in the USA, said it perfectly: **'sell the sizzle, not the steak'**.

A feature (the steak) is a statement of what you do or what something does. It forms the logical part of a decision-making process.

Therefore, both features (the steak) AND benefits (the sizzle) are important.

Here's the success formula ...

(FL + L + CB + CSM) = FAB

(Feature List + Link + Craft Benefit + Compelling Sales Message) = Features and Benefits

(FL) FEATURE LIST

First, you need to write a list of all the features of your service – all of them. Let me illustrate using a very simple example ... a common hole punch. These are some of the features you'd write down:

- – made of hardened steel

- – plastic cover on the base

- – removable base

- – plastic guide for your paper

(L) LINK

Then, to make the process of writing the corresponding benefits easier, use what's called a 'link'. Next to each feature write the words 'which means that'.

(CB) CRAFT BENEFIT

Now create the corresponding benefit.

I'll be honest with you, the first time you do this, you'll find it a challenge. But believe me it's worth the time and effort.

For example, here are three features:

- • self-setting clock

- • open 24 hours

- batteries included

Each is a feature, a factual statement about the product or service being promoted.

Let's look at the corresponding benefits of the features above.

- The benefit of a self-setting clock is convenience.

- The benefit of a store open 24 hours is that you can buy when you want.

- The benefit of batteries included is that the product is ready to use out of the box.

These may seem like true benefits, but we can go further. You should view your benefits as **'results'**.

The best way to understand the true benefit of your product or service is to answer the **'What's in it for me?'** question and to focus on results.

Let's take another look at that features list to see the possible benefits from the customer's point of view.

- Self-setting clock: I won't feel dumb!

- Open 24 hours: When my pregnant wife craves ice cream at 4 a.m., I won't have to disappoint her.

- Batteries included: I'll never have to see the look of disappointment on my child's face when their toy won't work because I forgot to buy batteries.

These may seem like true benefits, but we can go further. You should view your benefits as 'results' and communicate them as 'Compelling Sales Messages' ...

(CSM) Compelling Sales Message

The best way to understand the true benefit of your service is to answer the question 'What's in it for me?' and to focus on results and then communicate those results as Compelling Sales Messages.

Let's take another look at the first set of Features and Benefits of the common hole punch, to see the possible Compelling Sales Messages (in bold) from the Perfect Clients point of view ...

- Made of hardened steel so it will last forever, and **you'll never have to buy another one as long as you live.**

- The base has a plastic cover, so it collects all the punched-out paper and leaves no mess. **Your desk stays clean and scratch free no matter how often the punch is used.**

- The base is removable, so once the punch is full, you simply unclip the base and tip the waste into your bin. **It's easy to implement and leaves no mess.**

- The punch has a plastic guide for your paper, so you always punch the holes in the correct place, whatever the paper size. **You get perfect results every time.**

See the difference?

Once you've done that, you need to put each Feature/Benefit/Compelling Sales Message in order of importance, from most powerful to least powerful, and then communicate them as a bulleted list so they stand out (just as we discussed with your Lead Capture Pages).

Core Element #6: GUARANTEE

From my experience, hardly any service businesses offer a guarantee in their business. This is a BIG mistake.

A guarantee works at the point of purchase and is what I call a **'sales converter'** (discussed again in Chapter 7), but there are instances where you may use it in your tactics.

Therefore, applying a guarantee will increase leads and sales immediately. Yes, instantly!

Why do guarantees work so well?

As you know, the benefit of your service is gained after the sale is made, after you've acquired the customer. Sometimes this can be days, weeks, months or even years after the first sale was made (depending on what service you sell).

This in itself places a risk on the shoulders of would-be clients, customers or patients. It's this risk that often prevents them from buying or changing suppliers, even though they're not happy.

However, if you lower or eliminate this risk, then the natural consequence is that people will be more inclined to buy from you. Agreed?

That's the secret of creating a powerful guarantee that mitigates against the risk.

A guarantee is nothing more than simply taking away the barriers from the sale and ensures that the Perfect Client keeps progressing towards the sale.

As soon as you add a guarantee, it removes the risks of buying, ensuring more Perfect Clients are gained. It automatically differentiates your service business from the competition (if you recall, 'guarantee' is one of the eight 'differentiators' we discussed earlier), and it adds value.

Prospects will value your services much more, because they'll assume the service must live up to expectations, and the business must be excellent at delivering the service. ('Why would they offer a guarantee if the service wasn't great?').

The result is therefore a BIG increase in new leads and Perfect Clients!

The ultimate aim is to guarantee the result or main benefit of your service and add a 'penalty' should the service fail to live up to your promises.

Just to explain this further, here's a simple example of how risk reversal works. A man wants to buy a puppy for his daughter. He responds to two ads in the local newsagent's window. He examines the first puppy, and it seems ideal in temperament and looks. The owner says to the man, 'If the dog isn't right for your daughter, bring it back in a week, and I'll give you your money back.' Clearly, he appreciated the value of risk reversal and guarantees, but he didn't fully understand it!

The man then goes to look at the second puppy. Again, it seems ideal in temperament and looks, except that this time the owner says, 'Your daughter is obviously looking forward to her new puppy, and it's important that she's totally happy with it. Please take the puppy and let your daughter play with it, look after it and get to know it. If after three weeks the puppy is not right for her, bring the puppy back, and I'll refund your money in full and give you £50 for your time, effort and trouble.'

Now, this man really understands risk reversal. First, he extended the 'trial' period. He knows that his puppy is a good dog. He also knows that after three weeks the puppy and girl will be inseparable. He totally reverses the risk.

You also need to understand this … the company that reverses the risk, automatically gains a competitive advantage and wins more business, in fact, much more! This competitive advantage is very significant when attracting leads and Perfect Clients to your business.

Here's another example, one of the best I've ever seen. It's from a pest-control service company called BBBK. Their guarantee is aimed at hotels and restaurants. Just pretend, for a second, that you're a restaurateur and you have a problem with rodents. You're looking for a pest-control company, and you see the following guarantee:

```
You don't owe one penny until all the
pests on your premises have been
eradicated.

If you are ever dissatisfied with BBBK's
services, you will receive a refund for
up to 12 months of the company's
services … plus fees for another
```

exterminator of your choice for the next
year.

If a guest spots a pest on your
premises, BBBK will pay for the guest's
meal or room, send a letter of apology,
and pay for a future meal or stay … and
if your facility is closed down due to
the presence of roaches or rodents, BBBK
will pay any fines, as well as all lost
profits, plus $5000.

I defy you not to at least call them to find out more!

It's easy to assume several things about BBBK from this guarantee.

They are very good (the best?) at pest control.

They understand the concerns of their customers with regard to hygiene and the potentially damaging effects of any infestation.

They are very successful at attracting new clients!

They are probably providing very similar services to their competitors. However, they understand risk reversal and guarantees. Their profits reflect this!

In fact, some time ago Harvard Business School conducted a study around service business market share and included BBBK in the study and why it had such a large and disproportionate market share in North America. It concluded that their service guarantee was a key factor in gaining this market share over and above even the big players such as Rentokil.

Hopefully, you now have a basic grasp of guarantees and what they can achieve for your business. However, several questions may be entering your mind.

For example, 'Won't people try to abuse what I am offering?' and 'Won't I lose a lot of money with this?'

The key, of course, to successful guarantees is this: if you offer a good service (which you do), then you have nothing to worry about.

And ...

GUARANTEE ONLY WHAT <u>YOU</u> CONTROL

If you do that, you'll never have to worry about your guarantee. Yes, maybe one or two clients will take advantage of your guarantee, but the way to look at it is that the increase in leads and sales will far outweigh any refunds you have to give.

Therefore, you should be thinking about guaranteeing the results your services provide; guaranteeing delivery times on work; guaranteeing support services, you name it. Whatever you do and how you do it, you can guarantee it, and the bolder you are, the better.

One last point to mention is about adding 'conditions'. You should avoid adding conditions to the guarantee; otherwise, the guarantee is weakened.

Let's now look at the success formula ...

(GP + P) = G

(Guarantee the Promise + Punish the Business If Promise Not Delivered) = Guarantee

(GP) GUARANTEE THE PROMISE

The first thing you need to do is 'guarantee the promise'. In other words, identify the ultimate result that the Perfect Client is buying and then promise you will deliver on it.

For example, referring back to the differentiator Domino's Pizza used:

```
'Red hot pizza delivered to your door
    in 30 minutes or less, guaranteed'
```

Notice they guarantee the promise, which is to deliver 'red hot pizza in 30 minutes or less'.

(P) PUNISH THE BUSINESS IF PROMISE NOT DELIVERED

When you apply the first part of the success formula, it will immediately translate into more leads and sales. However, by adding this second part, your sales will increase even further.

What you need to do is 'punish' the business if it doesn't deliver the promised results.

For example, if Dominos don't deliver your pizza within 30 minutes, it's FREE.

If BBBK foul up, they refund the fees and pay for another exterminator, etc.

Be bold. Remember, if you're guaranteeing only what you control, you can be really confident! It will translate into many more leads and sales.

Core Element #7: REASONS WHY

When you use a sensational guarantee or an irresistible offer, or you make a statement that could be hard to believe, then if you don't back them up with reasons why, you'll lose leads and sales, because people will think 'it's too good to be true'.

The more sensational your irresistible offer (Crowd Puller) or guarantee, the more reasons you need to back it up with.

Therefore, you use 'reasons why' to validate and make your message sound believable.

This is actually very easy to apply. All you do is explain in simple and logical terms why you offer your guarantee or why you have an amazing offer.

Be honest.

There's no need to make it up.

For example, here's the guarantee for an estate agent:

`'If we don't sell your house within a week for the price we agree, we'll give you £500.'`

Here's the 'reasons why', word for word:

`'Why would we do this?`

`'It's quite simple really. Last year we sold 1817 houses, more than any other estate agent in Leicestershire. We're very good at it (read our testimonials).`

> 'But since you've never used us before
> to sell your home, we wanted to give you
> something that would put your mind at
> rest and reassure you that we can
> deliver (over-deliver) on our promises.
> That's why we offer this fantastic
> guarantee.'

Do you see what we're doing here? The 'reasons why' actually support and validate the guarantee and make it believable!

Let's look at the success formula ...

$$(R + A) = RW$$

(Rationale + Articulate) = Reasons Why

(R) RATIONALE

The best way to think about this is that you just need to justify WHY you're doing it or saying it.

For example, you could be the quickest at delivering X.

If that's the case, you need to explain WHY you're the quickest at delivering X.

Adding the rationale behind why you're the quickest makes it believable and, in fact, adds even more sales power.

Here's another example; it's the guarantee we offer with our MACHINE Done-For-You Programme ...

> If you don't believe the Systems Workshop is a
> life-changing day for you and your business,
> we'll refund 100% of your setup fees immediately.

(A) ARTICULATE

You then simply need to articulate the rationale so it makes sense and completely overcomes any cynicism or doubts in the mind of your customer or potential customer.

And here are the reasons why for The Mentors Guild (one of our membership programmes for coaches, consultants and mentors) ...

All we're really asking you to say is 'maybe'. Don't risk a single penny or cent with our unconditional 30-day, money-back GUARANTEE.

The guarantee is in place to give you complete peace of mind.

We know how good membership of The Mentors Guild is, and the guarantee shows we stand by it 100%.

Join today, and if within the first 30 days, for any reason, you want to cancel, simply let us know, and we'll refund every single penny you've paid. We can't be fairer than that!

Core Element #8: SOCIAL PROOF

What further supports your message and proves that you do deliver on your promises is the use of something that's known as *social proof.*

Social proof is a term used to describe a set of credibility builders. The more credibility you have in your sales and marketing, the more believable and trustworthy it all becomes, and that instantly translates into transformed results.

Credibility builders include …

- videos, comments, reviews and testimonials from Perfect Clients;

- case studies;

- membership of credible associations;

- industry awards, etc.

The more you include, the better.

Once again, the more aligned to your Perfect Clients it is, the more powerful your social proof will be.

For example, if your target market is businesses who turnover £250k to £500k, the only testimonials you should be using are from businesses of a similar size.

If you sell to the affluent, then your case studies should be from affluent clients advocating your service.

I cannot overstate the importance of this. Relevance is a key motivator, so the more relevant your social proof (and everything else!) is to your Perfect Clients, the more appealing you'll become to them.

Think about your own purchasing decisions. Isn't it more comforting to know other people just like you are pleased with their experience with the business selling the product or service.

How often do you book a holiday or hotel without looking at the online reviews from customers? How influential is a bad comment and, conversely, a good comment?

Review sites are becoming more and more important, and 'Reputation Marketing' (as it's now called) is playing a significant role, especially online, in purchasing decisions. That's social proof.

As you can see, testimonials play a big part in convincing your Perfect Clients that others have tried your service, and that they have had a good experience.

Ideally, your testimonials should stress a number of your key benefits. The more positive the reinforcement of your overall offer, the better.

You may think getting client testimonials is challenging. It's not. Simply write to your Perfect Clients and ask them to give you a few comments or, ideally, a video about what they like about your business and your services, and ask for their permission to use their video and comments on your material. You'll be surprised at the responses you get and how good the comments are.

Then, once you've got your supply of testimonials, simply use the ones which convey your benefits best. It really is that simple!

Let's take a look at the success formula ...

(CB + C) = SP

(Credibility Builders + Communicate) = Social Proof

(CB) CREDIBILITY BUILDERS

Your task here is simple. Create and develop as many credibility builders (listed above) as possible. As I said, the more, the better.

(C) COMMUNICATE

Once you've collected your credibility builders, you need to then add them and communicate them in your tactics.

Core Element #9: CALL TO ACTION

And finally, in all your tactics you must use a powerful Call to Action. You'll find this easy having already identified your *primary objective*. Your Call to Action is created to ensure as many Perfect Clients as possible take immediate action and fulfil your primary objective!

But let's be clear ...

Getting anyone to DO something isn't easy. More often than not, your Perfect Client is busy. Other things are demanding their attention. In fact, responding is usually not convenient, and they need to be pushed to take action.

The late, great copywriter Gary Halbert said, 'you should pretend your prospect is a huge sloth of a man sitting in his chair'.

To get him to move an inch requires enormous effort. Your tactics must be powerful enough to get him out of his comfortable seat and respond.

It's very easy for your prospect to say to themselves, 'I'll reply tomorrow.' But, as we all know, tomorrow often never comes!

Therefore, your number-one goal is to get your Perfect Prospects to act now.

Your Call to Action is all-important in achieving this. Tests have proved that without a Call to Action your sales and marketing is likely to be 50% less effective. That's how important the Call to Action is.

Yet it's missing from most tactics I see.

A Call to Action isn't just adding your phone number or landing page URL to the bottom or top of an ad or letter or any other tactic you're using.

You literally have to tell your recipient what to do next.

Again, this is very simple to do, especially when you've already identified your primary objective.

If you want them to go to your Lead Capture Page, you'd say something like this:

```
Simply click on this link, and you'll go straight
to our website. From there, you can immediately
download our FREE special report titled, 'How to
Create a Thick, Lush Green Lawn 12 Months of the
Year'. Remember, the report is FREE until 13
June, so go and get it now.
```

Do you see how easy this is?

Let's put it all together with the success formula ...

(SO + SR + MR +WHN) = CTA

(Summarise the Offer + Stimulator Reminder + Multiple Ways of Responding + What Happens Next) = Call to Action

(SO) SUMMARISE THE OFFER

The first thing you need to do is to Summarise the Offer. Tell them what they will get when they respond.

For example:

```
To download our FREE special report detailing the
'Seven Secrets to Saving Five Figures in Tax' …
```

(SR) STIMULATOR REMINDER

Next, remind them why they need to respond now (your 'Stimulator'):

```
Remember, download our FREE special report
detailing the 'Seven Secrets to Saving Five
Figures in Tax' within the next four days …
```

(MR) MULTIPLE WAYS OF RESPONDING

Then, give them more than one way to respond (unless you have good reason for offering just one way of responding). People have preferred ways of responding and buying. The more options you give, the better your results will be.

```
Remember, download our FREE special report
detailing the 'Seven Secrets to Saving Five
Figures in Tax' within the next four days. Simply
go to www.abc.com or call us on 0800 123 456 …
```

(WHN) WHAT HAPPENS NEXT

Finally, tell them what will happen when they respond.

Remember, download our FREE special report detailing the 'Seven Secrets to Saving Five Figures in Tax' within the next four days. Simply go to www.abc.com, or call us on 0800 123 456. You'll then be able to apply each of the strategies and secrets to your own business, resulting in huge savings in tax. Do it now.

*****

Okay. Those are the nine Core Elements. I promise that as soon as you start applying them to all your tactics, you'll see a remarkable and instant uplift in results.

Remember, adding or improving each of the Core Elements doesn't cost you a single penny. You're using the Core Elements to make your tactics work more effectively.

Go through all your existing tactics and, one-by-one, add the Core Elements to them.

Then, when you add any new tactics, make sure the Core Elements are included in them.

It's impossible NOT to transform your results when you do this.

You're on your way now. You now know what you need to include, no matter what tactic you're using in any of the three Media Channels.

But before moving on, let me explain how you then tailor the use of the Core Elements to the channels and tactics you're using, because, as I said, there are nuances with each of the three Media Channels and their corresponding tactics.

Once you've grasped this, it doesn't matter what tactics you're producing, on what platform or in what Media Channel ... they are guaranteed to work ...

Tailoring the Core Elements to Your Tactics

You now have a thorough understanding of what it takes to get your tactics to perform, maybe for the first time.

And, as I've just said, no matter what Media Channel you're using and no matter what the tactic is, you simply apply the Core Elements to it, and results will improve.

But depending on the tactic you're using, you may not have the space to apply all nine Core Elements. Plus, you may choose NOT to use some of them, depending where you are in your system.

For example, let's talk about space or, more specifically, lack of space ...

If you're running text ads in LinkedIn, you get one image, 25 characters for the headline and 175 characters for the description.

But if you're running a LinkedIn InMail campaign (email delivered to a Perfect Clients LinkedIn Inbox) you have no restriction on the character length.

If you're running a YouTube In-Stream campaign your video has no restriction ... it can be as long as you want it to be.

But if you're running Google Ads, once again you have strict controls in terms of the number of characters you can use for the headings and descriptions.

If you're running classified ads in a publication or even a full-page ad, you may not have space to include all nine Core Elements.

The same goes with using, say, a postcard. But if you're using a letter, you have no restrictions in terms of space.

So, use this approach when space or time (if using video) is restricted ...

Always call out your Perfect Clients. Always lead with a headline. Always have a Call to Action. That's the minimum requirement.

Then, if space or time allow, use your common sense to decide what other Core Elements to include.

And, as I said, you also need to consider where you are in your system. If your Crowd Puller is your FREE Special Report, and that's the focus of your Lead Capture Page, it's unlikely you'll need to use your guarantee at this stage.

But if your Crowd Puller is your book, and at the very least you're asking people to pay for 'shipping and handling', then you should definitely offer a money-back guarantee on the book.

Launching Your Tactics

As I mentioned previously, you should first use the Core Elements to optimise everything you're currently doing to maximise the number of leads you're getting. Then, start adding one tactic at a time across the three Media Channels.

But what you must NOT do is plough everything into your tactics and risk losing your hard-earned money.

So, when using a tactic that has a cost, it's imperative you minimise your financial risk to begin with (I call this the 'Minimum Risk Formula') and then, once it's working, increase your spend gradually and scale up.

I'll talk in detail about this later in Chapter 11, but I just wanted to draw your attention to it at this point so you don't go all out without putting in place sensible precautions.

Putting It All Together

Your Lead Generation System is a pivotal cog in THE MACHINE. It drives your Conversion System and your Maximising Client Value System, and, as you'll see later, it will be one of the biggest levers you have when it comes to scaling your service business too.

Your Lead Generation System is the lifeblood of THE MACHINE, YOUR MACHINE, so it's important you carefully apply each step, and when you do that, you'll have a truly amazing system for generating high-quality leads from your Perfect Clients.

But the best Lead Generation System in the world is worth nothing if you don't convert those leads into clients. Let's take a look at how you do that ...

Chapter Summary

- There are four steps in any successful Lead Generation System ...

  1. The Crowd Puller.
  2. Lead Capture Page.
  3. The Media Circle.
  4. Message To Market.

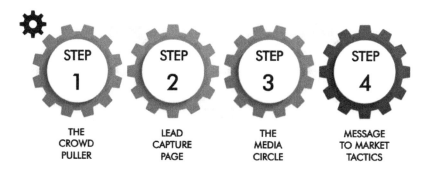

- There are three very successful Crowd Pullers ...

  5. Special Report.
  6. Webinar.
  7. Book.

- You'll get the best results when you use all three Crowd Pullers.

- Your Lead Capture Page is structured to ensure a high percentage of visitors (Perfect Clients) convert into a lead.

- There are three (not one) Media Channels that make up the Media Circle ...

1. E-Media.
2. P-Media.
3. DM-Media.

- You should use all three channels, or at least two of them, to reach your Perfect Clients.

- Use The Advanced Precision Targeting Model to laser focus on your Perfect Clients.

- The nine Core Elements ensure your tactics are successful.

- You'll transform the results of ALL your existing and future tactics when you apply the Core Elements.

- Identify the primary objective of your tactic before adding any of the Core Elements. Your tactic must be focused on getting as many Perfect Clients as you can to take action and fulfil the primary objective.

- Nine Core Elements ...

1. **Perfect Client**

2. **Differentiator:**
   Success Formula: $(U + C + CC) = D$
   (Unique + Create Uniqueness+ Craft and Communicate)
   = Differentiator

3. **Headline:**
   Success Formula: $(HT + T + F) = H$
   (Headline Template + Test Before Launch + Format) = Headline

4. Irresistible Offer:

Success Formula: (D + S + C) = IO

(Desire + Stimulator + Communicate) = Irresistible Offer

5. Features and Benefits:

Success Formula: (FL + L + CB + CSM) = FAB

(Feature List + Link + Craft Benefit + Compelling Sales Message) = Features and Benefits

6. Guarantee:

Success Formula: (GP + P) = G

(Guarantee the Promise + Punish the Business If Promise Not Delivered) = Guarantee

7. Reasons Why:

Success Formula: (R + A) = RW

(Rationale + Articulate) = Reasons Why

8. Social Proof:

Success Formula: (CB + C) = SP

(Credibility Builders + Communicate) = Social Proof

9. Call To Action:

Success Formula: (SO + SR + MR + 203HEN) = CTA

(Summarise the Offer + Stimulator Reminder + Multiple Ways of Responding + What Happens Next) = Call to Action

THE MACHINE

CHAPTER 7

CONVERSION SYSTEM

The Conversion System is the second part of the Growth Continuum ...

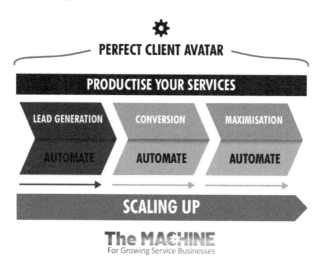

Let me start by telling you a story of how I came to get a full grasp of how you can really influence the chances of converting leads into clients ...

THE MACHINE

When I was thinking of joining Leicester Tigers way back in 1990, something happened that has stayed with me forever. It's a valuable story that you can benefit from right now, too.

I was at work when Michelle, our receptionist, called me to say a chap by the name of Tony Russ was on the phone. A year earlier, while still at Loughborough University, I had played for England Students, where Tony was the coach, so I knew him well. Tony, was also head coach at Leicester Tigers and the first-ever full-time, fully paid coach in world rugby. I had no idea why he was calling.

He said, 'Steve, I'll cut to the chase. I've obviously seen you playing for Nottingham (I played for Nottingham prior to joining Tigers), and we had worked more closely together with England Students the previous season. I want you to come to Leicester Tigers.'

That conversation started the ball rolling in terms of me leaving Nottingham.

Tony asked me to think about it, which I did. He said he'd call back in a week.

And what happened next is one of the most valuable lessons I've ever had when it comes to nurturing leads and converting them into clients.

When Tony called back (as he promised he would) I told him I was interested (I'm a 'lead' now), but I had some doubts and a lot of questions. He replied, 'Look Steve, why don't you come to the Club, where we can chat over lunch, and I can answer any questions you have.'

About a week later I went to see Tony, but, prior to the meeting, Tony sent me an agenda. It detailed everything we would be covering. It was very impressive. It included a tour around the ground and the facilities, the vision of the Club, and various other things.

When we met, Tony talked about building a team that would rival the best in Europe. And what really impressed me in addition was that Tony had organised various key people at the Club to join us at different times throughout the meeting. First, Peter Wheeler, Club Chairman and legend of the sport, met with me to reinforce what Tony was saying. Then, Les Cusworth popped in to talk about me joining the Club and what it would do for my game (I would subsequently work with Pete and Les at P&G Bland, the insurance brokers I mentioned earlier in the book). At the time, Les was also assistant England coach (to Jack Rowell), and I knew him well, as we had played together a few years before for the Midlands, plus, of course, I was also in the England setup. Les told me in no uncertain way how much it would help my game if I joined Tigers.

And then Dean Richards turned up. Dean was captain of the first team and a Tigers and England superstar. Dean was a policeman at the time (rugby union wouldn't turn professional for another five years). He came into Tony's office in his police uniform and again told me how much the Club wanted me and what he and Tony were looking to put in place.

Dean took me on a tour of the ground (which was very impressive). It was, and still is, one of the finest rugby stadiums on the planet. As an ambitious rugby player, it was impossible not to be impressed. Back then rugby was a much smaller sport than it is now. The average crowd for the likes of Nottingham (where I was playing) and Bath, then the top English Premiership teams, was around five or six thousand. Tigers on the other hand, would regularly get twelve to fifteen thousand. In terms of atmosphere when you are playing, I can tell you first-hand that the difference those extra seven thousand fans make, is huge.

Back then, however, Tigers' training facilities were like every other rugby club: poor. In fact, their gym was the size of a postage stamp and housed under one of the stands. But Tony showed me the plans of their new training facility at Oval Park. It was a stand-alone training facility about five miles from the stadium, destined in twelve months to become the finest rugby union training facility in the world. It included a state-of-the-art gym, all-weather pitches, and so on. Whereas this type of facility is commonplace now, back then Tigers were at the forefront of player development. Tony reeled off the coaching team he had assembled, including the dieticians, speed coaches, and so on. Remember, although having a support team such as this is the norm these days, back then this approach was revolutionary. It was way ahead of its time and even legions ahead of football (soccer), which had been a professional sport in the UK for decades. Yet when it came to player development and training, soccer was simply back in the dark ages.

It was impossible for me not to be extremely impressed.

Then Tony said, 'Steve, obviously this is not just your decision. I know Helen (Helen was my girlfriend at the time, but

Tony had met her during our England Student games) needs to be comfortable with the Club, too.' Again, this may not seem such a big thing, but I can tell you back then rugby was such a male-dominated sport (thankfully, it's not now) that for someone to even consider one's partner in the decision-making process was nigh on revolutionary! Tony went on to ask, 'Steve, can we organise to bring Helen to the Club and show her around, too?'

What Tony was doing was making sure all the relevant decision-makers (stakeholders) were being considered.

It was a highly impressive 'courtship', and because of what Tony planned and the people he brought in to meet me, it demonstrated to me that they really cared about the players, their wives or partners, and that THEY WANTED ME.

After that process, it was simply impossible to say 'no'.

Was this a one-off?

No, it wasn't.

That approach was responsible for building one of the finest club rugby teams ever assembled, and one that would go on to dominate European and English club rugby for the best part of 20 years.

Tony had implemented a number of powerful steps that he knew would have a major effect and influence on my decision-making process. From the first phone call, then the impactful agenda, right through to getting Helen involved in the decision-making process … it was all beautifully choreographed.

And the type of approach that Tony had put in place to 'convert' me is exactly what you need to do when it comes to converting YOUR leads into sales.

Put a series of steps in place that make it impossible for the lead NOT to become a client.

Very simply, you need a system that starts the moment the lead is generated and finishes once they become a client.

I call this a 'Conversion System' and it's missing from most established service businesses I come across.

But it's not JUST about acquiring the client.

Arguably even more important is acquiring the client at the *RIGHT* fee .... and it may surprise you to learn that everything we've covered so far in this book has been with that in mind.

It doesn't take skill to give your services and expertise away cheaply. The skill is to get clients at the fee YOU want.

And that's why I've taken the time so far to give you the platform for achieving that.

Let me take you through the Conversion System you need to put in place.

Figure 7.1 shows a high-level view of it.

Remember, it needs to start the moment the lead is generated ... and finish only once the client is acquired at the right fee ...

Figure 7.1. The Conversion System

The great news is that your Conversion System costs very little to put in place.

It consists of at least seven strategic steps, choreographed to effortlessly guide the Perfect Client from being a lead into a client paying the right fee.

Every step you put in place should be systemised, and once in place, ALL the non-human steps should be automated (which we'll discuss in Chapter 9).

Once in play, you'll be able to tweak each step of the system so it produces the best possible results for you. Remember, the goal is simple ...

To convert as many leads as you can into clients, at the right fee.

Now, unlike your Lead Generation System, which has pre-defined steps, your Conversion System, in the main, very much depends on what services you sell and how you sell them.

So, I'll explain how to create a Conversion System that's perfect for you.

First, let me explain why your Conversion System must have at least seven steps ...

The chart shown in Figure 7.2 is based on research conducted by Thomas Publishing but is backed-up by many other studies that have been carried out over the last couple of decades.

As you can see, it shows how many points of contact (follow-up steps once a lead is generated) are required, on average, with a supplier before a sale is made.

Obviously, people can buy after one or two contacts, but at seven contacts, 94% of people buy. Interestingly, the research also shows that most businesses are very poor when it comes to follow-up and most give up. In fact, almost 80% have stopped following up after the third point of contact.

Therefore, to give yourself the best possible chance of getting the sale, your Conversion System must have at least seven steps, or, as I call them, seven points of contact.

That gives you two distinct advantages ...

Firstly, your Conversion System is benefiting from the fact that you'll get more sales simply by having at least seven points of contact in it.

Secondly, if you're in a competitive situation where your Perfect Clients are also looking at your competitors, in all likelihood they won't have a follow-up system that extends beyond three points of contact, so it will be just you in play who's following up with them, again ensuring you get more sales.

*Figure 7.2. How Many Points of Contact Does It Take
Before a Sale Is Made?*

The next question is what do you do at each point of contact? More importantly, what do you do so that each point of contact has a positive influence on your Perfect Clients and moves them closer to the sale?

The good news is that when you're armed with what I'm about to reveal to you, it makes it so much easier, and, in fact,

EVERY step in your Conversion System will be inderpinned by it.

I can tell you this is arguably one of the most significant findings I have made over the last 25 years or so when it comes to converting leads into sales.

It's called 'Moments of Truth' (in addition to using it for your Conversion System, you'll also use it once the client is acquired).

Let me explain all about it ...

In 1987, Jan Carlzon, CEO of Scandinavian Airlines (SAS), wrote the book *Moments of Truth*. It explained how he took the airline from deficit to profit by 'moving' the airline to a world-class, customer-focused organisation.

Now, as you know, there have been many books written on customer service, but where this book and Carlzon's strategies really differ is his focus on each individual interaction the customer has with the business. He calls these **Moments of Truth**, and, of course, each interaction can be a positive or a negative experience.

As I said, like Carlzon advises, you will be using Moments of Truth for your clients, but I've found that it's equally as powerful to base your entire Conversion System on Moments of Truth.

You see, because Moments of Truth work on every individual interaction, it's perfect for every point of contact in your Conversion System.

Take a look at the diagram shown in Figure 7.3. It shows how, at each point of contact (Moment of Truth), you need to ensure each interaction is a favourable one for the Perfect Client.

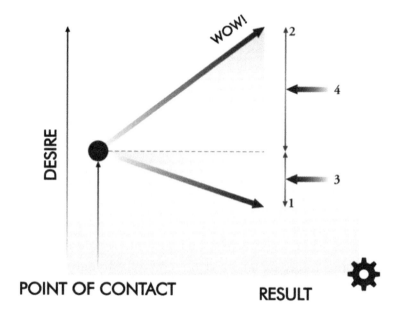

POINT OF CONTACT   **RESULT**

Legend
1. The effect on the Perfect Client when the business doesn't actively focus on each interaction with them. Notice the Moment of Truth was a negative experience, reducing the prospect's desire and therefore creating discontent (no matter how small).
2. Moments of Truth approach. By breaking down each point of contact to ensure an excellent experience, the desire level is raised even higher.
3. Shows the drop in desire when a business doesn't focus on each point of contact.
4. Shows the increase in desire gained by using Moments of Truth.

Figure 7.3. Moments of Truth

So, at each step in your Conversion System, this is the effect you're trying to achieve.

At the very least, you want every step in your Conversion System to be above the dotted line. That means it's a positive experience, but the higher above this line, the better.

Once I've explained exactly how to use Moments of Truth, you'll also be able to create what I call 'WOW! Moments'. These are points of contact that make the prospective client think you're amazing. On the Moments of Truth diagram, a WOW! Moment is at point 2. It's the highest Moment of Truth experience you can achieve.

Let's take a second or two to summarise ...

You're going to create a Conversion System with at least seven steps that's choreographed around Moments of Truth. You're going to create at least one WOW! Moment across that system, and every step is going to be positive for the Perfect Client.

Now, let me show you how to put a Conversion System in place that's perfect for your service business ...

Creating a Conversion System

STEP 1: Existing conversion optimisation

The first thing to do is review what you currently have in place which takes a lead and turns it into a client.

Add any missing Core Elements (detailed earlier) and make sure they are all being used optimally. Although it is important to apply ALL the Core Elements, the following two

Core Elements will significantly contribute to increasing conversion:

- guarantee
- social proof

This simple process of improving your existing conversion will enable you to get quick increases in sales without any extra expense.

STEP 2: Map the stages of the conversion system to create your Framework.

To create the high-level steps of your Conversion System, simply use the 'Conversion System Framework Table' shown in Figure 7.4. To make things even easier for you, you can download the actual document from here:

www.themachine.co.uk/book-resources

Notice the very bottom row of the Framework is titled 'Maximising Client Value System'. As you can see, this starts once the Perfect Client has been acquired and is covered in the next chapter.

Simply use the table to first map the key STAGES that have to occur as part of your Conversion System. A stage could be any of the following:

- a meeting at your offices or online;
- a form received;
- a visit to the client;
- etc.

DAY	POINT OF CONTACT	OBJECTIVE
	LEAD GENERATED	
	STAGE 1: Expertise-Based Irresistible Offer	
0		
	STAGE 2: Response Mechanics	
0		
	STAGE 3: <Enter Details>	
0		
	STAGE 4: <Enter Details>	
0		
	STAGE 5: <Enter Details>	
0		
	STAGE 6: <Enter Details>	
0		
	SALE & NEW CLIENT ACQUIRED	
	MAXIMISING CLIENT VALUE SYSTEM	

Figure 7.4. Conversion System Framework Table

The system starts the moment the lead is generated and ends when the sale is made. By adding the key stages between these two points, you've created the 'Framework'.

You may even find it easier to get a sheet of paper, turn it so it's landscape, then draw a horizontal line from the left to the right. On the far left write 'Lead Generated', and on the far right, write 'Client Acquired'.

Notice the first two stages are set. Irrespective of the service business you run, you will always have these first two stages as the first two stages of YOUR Conversion System (I'll explain why shortly).

You may have any number of stages in your Framework.

Note, there will be multiple points of contact at each stage. Simply include all of them in the 'Stages' rows in chronological order in the Conversion Framework Table.

Let's say I run an accounting firm; my key Framework stages would be:

1. Expertise-Based Irresistible Offer.

2. Response mechanics.

3. Meeting arranged at my offices.

4. Reception greeting.

5. The meeting.

6. Post-meeting.

Figure 7.5 shows how that looks in my table.

DAY	POINT OF CONTACT	OBJECTIVE
	LEAD GENERATED	
	STAGE 1: Expertise-Based Irresistible Offer	
0		
	STAGE 2: Response Mechanics	
0		
	STAGE 3: Meeting Arranged	
0		
	STAGE 4: Reception Greeting	
0		
	STAGE 5: The Meeting	
0		
	STAGE 6: Post Meeting	
0		
	SALE & NEW CLIENT ACQUIRED	
	MAXIMISING CLIENT VALUE SYSTEM	

Figure 7.5. The Stages in an Accountants Framework

Before we move on to Step 3, let me take a little time to explain the importance of your 'Expertise-Based Irresistible Offer' and 'Response Mechanics' ...

Expertise-Based Irresistible Offer

This is arguably the most important stage in your Conversion System and a stage missing from most businesses.

If your Crowd Puller is either a FREE Special Report or book, as you can see in Figure 7.6, then the first stage of your Conversion System must be what I call your 'Expertise-Based Irresistible Offer' ...

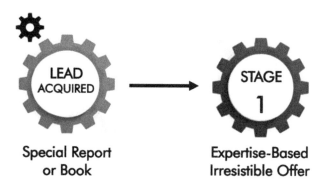

Figure 7.6. The Expertise-Based Irresistible Offer Is Always the First Step After Your Special Report or Book Is Requested

Ideally, this should be delivered via a video. There are four important elements of the video ...

1. Thank the Perfect Client for requesting the Crowd Puller, and then explain the virtues of it and why it's so useful and beneficial for them.

2. Next, reinforce your expertise. Tell them about your productised service and how you've created it to help them specifically. Tell them how it solves their problems. How it benefits them and why it's so unique.

3. Then deliver your irresistible offer. This, of course, depends on the service you're selling. If it doesn't require a face-to-face meeting to sell it, then you should give them an offer they can't refuse to buy your service right there and then. On the other hand, if selling your service requires a meeting of some kind, then make sure you tell them that the meeting is free, and even though it's free you still need to 'sell' it. Explain what they'll get out of the meeting. Explain how your specific expertise will help them during the meeting. Explain why meeting with you is going to be so beneficial to them.

4. And finally, reinforce the next step you want them to take. Tell them they can either buy your service right now and take advantage of your irresistible offer, or complete an application and then book a meeting via your online diary (more on this later).

Putting in place an Expertise-Based Irresistible Offer right after a Perfect Client enters their details to get your Crowd Puller will give you an instant uplift in sales or meetings, even before they receive or read your Special Report or book!

Response Mechanics

I'm sure you've heard the saying 'strike while the iron's hot'. This is absolutely crucial when it comes to converting leads into clients.

Getting this right could literally be the difference between your conversions going through the roof or falling flat ... and so many service businesses get this wrong.

It also explains why the Expertise-Based Irresistible Offer works so well. Your Perfect Clients are at their hottest right at the start of this journey. Your job is to keep them hot as they go through your Conversion System. In fact, what I'm taking you through is exactly what you need to do to get them even hotter so they find it impossible not to buy from you. But if you don't deal with your Perfect Prospects correctly once they register for your Crowd Puller, they'll quickly go cold, and you'll lose any chance you had to get the sale.

Speed is key. For example, if someone calls in making an enquiry, it must be dealt with immediately. We've tested this to finite levels and even waiting 30 minutes to get back to a prospective client significantly reduces your chances of a sale. It doesn't matter whether you sell high- or low-ticket services, speed is crucial.

And think about it ...

You want to not only strike while the iron is hot but also prevent them from using a competitor instead. By putting in place a Conversion System you are significantly improving your chances of blowing the competition out of the water, but you have to be in the game to affect the outcome. Responding slowly puts you out of the game and explains why many opportunities fall by the wayside.

Response Mechanics is a small part of this book, but honestly, it's one of the most important elements, because it has a major effect on your ability to acquire more (or fewer!) clients.

Just remember ... speed wins ... ALWAYS!

STEP 3: Decide how many points of contact you require.

Now you have your Framework in place, you need to decide on the number of contacts between each of the stages.

As a guide, the higher the price of your services and/or the longer the sales cycle (i.e. the average time it takes for a prospect to move to the next Stage), the more points of contact you'll want to build in. But remember, no matter what, it is important you build in at least seven points of contact.

Your points of contact go in the 'Points of Contact' column of the Framework table. Using my example of an accounting firm, here are the points of contact I would include:

STAGE 1: Expertise-Based Irresistible Offer

- *Point of Contact #1:* After opting in to Crowd Puller, Perfect Client redirected to Expertise-Based Irresistible Offer page with video.

- *Point of Contact #2:* Expertise-Based Follow-Up Campaign sent to people who do not progress to Stage 2.

STAGE 2: Response Mechanics

- *Point of Contact #3:* Receive inbound phone call or make out-bound call (depending on how the lead was generated).

- *Point of Contact #4:* Partner speaks to prospect.

Please note that it is very important at this stage to make sure that when the initial lead comes in, you collect any other additional details from the prospect. If you're going to use email, SMS texts and mail, for example, if you haven't already done so, you must get the email address, mobile number and postal address of the prospect.

STAGE 3: Meeting Arranged

- Email details of meeting (send agenda, directions and parking instructions).

- Send confirmation letter.

- Send Surprise Package prior to meeting (this may include video testimonials, a couple of Special Reports and a personalised welcome video from the partner further introducing themselves to the prospect and telling them they are looking forward to the meeting).

STAGE 4: Reception Greeting

- Receptionist greets prospect by name when they arrive.

- Offer refreshments (use 'Drinks Menu').

- Partner also greets prospect in person.

STAGE 5: The Meeting

- Follow meeting sales process (use multiple presentation aids).

- Ask for the order.

STAGE 6: Post-Meeting

- Meeting follow-up letter;
- Phone call;
- Follow-up system.

Notice that because you're now taking a strategic approach to your Conversion System, you can add elements you believe will enhance the Perfect Client journey from a lead to a client, customer or patient. Think about the points of contact you can add that will have a positive effect on the Perfect Client bringing them closer to the sale.

Figure 7.7 shows how this now looks in my table.

STEP 4: Write down the objective of each contact.

This is imperative. Every contact has to have an objective. There are two types of objectives you need to think about:

1. Courtesy objectives: For example, thanking the Perfect Client and informing them of what will happen next.

    Here's an email you could send:

    Subject: Thank you, John

    Hi John,

    I just wanted to say thank you for arranging the Suitability Meeting at <Date and time> (your Zoom login details are below).

    I look forward to meeting you and explaining how <insert differentiator>.

DAY	POINT OF CONTACT	OBJECTIVE
	LEAD GENERATED	
	STAGE 1: Expertise-Based Irresistible Offer	
0	Expertise-Based Irresistible Offer Video	
	Conversion Follow-Up Sequence	
	STAGE 2: Response Mechanics	
0	Receive in-bound form or call (or make out-bound call)	
	Partner speaks with prospect	
	STAGE 3: Meeting Arranged	
0	Email details of meeting	
	Send confirmation letter	
	Send Surprise Package	
	STAGE 4: Reception Greeting	
0	Receptionist greets prospect	
	Offer refreshments	
	Partner greets prospect	
	STAGE 5: The Meeting	
0	Follow meeting sales process	
	Ask for the order	
	STAGE 6: Post Meeting	
0	Meeting follow-up letter	
	Follow-up phone call	
	Follow-up system	
	SALE & NEW CLIENT ACQUIRED	
	MAXIMISING CLIENT VALUE SYSTEM	

Figure 7.7. Points of Contact Added

227

```
Thanks again, John.

Kind regards,

Julie Jones
Managing Director
```

2. <u>Next step objectives</u>. For example, if the Perfect Client didn't go ahead at the Suitability Meeting, your subsequent follow-ups would have the objective of getting the Perfect Client to buy your services.

   Having already constructed your Framework (made up from each stage), the objective is easy.

   It is simply to get the prospect to reach the next stage in your Conversion System.

   Add the objective to the table in the 'Objective Column'.

STEP 5: Add Timeline

Now, for each contact, simply decide on when the contact will occur. Day 0 means the contact happens the same day as the Critical Stage is reached.

Day 3 means the contact is delivered three days after the stage was reached, and so on.

Once a Critical Stage is reached the timeline starts again at zero.

STEP 6: Decide the exact nature of each Point of Contact and create.

Decide what each contact will consist of.

What will you include?

What will you say?

For example, my initial confirmation email, may look something like this:

```
Subject: Our meeting …

Good afternoon, Akash.

I'm just writing to confirm our meeting at
our offices on 21 November at 10 a.m.

I have also written to you today with
further details including an Agenda and
directions.

If you have any questions before our meeting
please email me on:

>> steve@abcaccountants.com

   … or call me on <Telephone Number>.

Thanks again, Akash. I'm looking forward to
meeting you.

Kind regards,

Steve Hackney

Partner
```

STEP 7: Add the Core Elements where you can.

Steps 1–6 take you through the procedure you need to follow to put your actual Conversion System in place.

Now, you're going to look at each point of contact and add, where relevant, as many of the Core Elements as you can.

The more you add, the higher your conversion will be.

For example, if you need some kind of sales meeting, then make sure you have a list of social proofs to show the prospect, add a powerful guarantee and give them an irresistible offer they can't refuse.

Trust me, when you add the power of the Core Elements and sprinkle them throughout your Conversion System, you're going to enjoy results like you've never seen before.

STEP 8: Keep following up to take advantage of 'The Moving Parade'.

Selling any service (or product) is all about timing. Just because someone isn't interested in buying your service today, it doesn't mean they aren't going to be interested tomorrow.

That is, in essence, what 'The Moving Parade' is all about. Let me explain this further.

Let's say that at the moment you're really happy with your car. You've got no intention of changing it. Therefore, every online or offline advert, every email, every mailing or any contact you have with a car dealer or car manufacturer is wasted on you.

You glance at any online ads and quickly move on. Letters go in the bin without a second thought. You pick up your mobile when the adverts come on TV. You simply aren't interested. And nothing will prompt you at this stage to even consider changing your car. However, three months later your circumstances have changed. You need to do more travelling, and so you decide it's time to look for a more suitable car.

Now, online and offline adverts, every mailing and every communication to do with cars is instantly gets your attention. You're 'in the market' for a new car, and you develop an insatiable appetite to find out as much as you can about the cars which would suit you best.

This happens every single day when people are buying products and services. If you don't keep in touch regularly with your Perfect Clients, you'll never get 'lucky' with the timing. People move in and out of 'buying mode', depending on their changing circumstances. Figure 7.8 shows how it looks.

By keeping in contact at least once a month (even better results are gained by having a weekly follow-up regime), the chances that you will hit the Perfect Client at the right time are increased tenfold. You WILL get 'LUCKY'!

This one strategy will see your results improve overnight. Taking advantage of The Moving Parade is one of the simplest, most profitable business growth strategies you can apply to your service business.

Step 9: Monitor, test and improve

Once your Conversion System is operating, you can measure, test and improve the results of each contact. I discuss this in detail in Chapter 12.

People/Businesses Who Aren't in a Position to Buy – AT THE MOMENT
These people outside the 'Buying Mode' circle are in your Perfect Client target group but for a number of reasons will not buy at the moment.

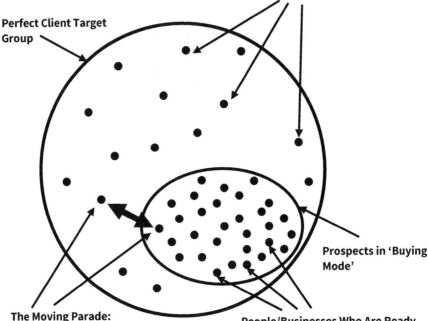

Perfect Client Target Group

Prospects in 'Buying Mode'

The Moving Parade: People/Businesses That Either Become Buyers or Non-Buyers
People or businesses move in and out of 'buying mode' all the time. Circumstances change, resulting in people or businesses either becoming buyers or non-buyers. This movement in and out of 'buying mode' is what I call The Moving Parade.

People/Businesses Who Are Ready to Buy Right Now
These people inside the 'Buying Mode' circle are ready to buy right now. Remember, they can buy from only YOU or your competitors.

Figure 7.8. The Moving Parade

Conclusion

This may well be the first time you've seen anything like this for converting leads into sales.

Believe me, this is extremely powerful and costs very little to put in place.

Even if you have a short sales cycle, you'll be able to build in powerful points of contact that demonstrate to the Perfect Client that you would be a great business to buy from (or keep buying from).

This may seem to be a very manual-based system to put in place, but don't worry. I'll deal with this in Chapter 9, when I talk to you about system automation.

Okay. You've identified your Perfect Clients. You've Productised Your Services. You've added a Lead Generation System and created a beautifully choreographed Conversion System. Now let's look at the most lucrative part of your business, one that in my experience is neglected by almost every established service business: maximising the value of your clients, customers or patients ...

Chapter Summary

- Concentrating on converting more leads into clients, customers, or patients will ensure two things:

  1. You'll transform your service business overnight.
  2. You'll maximise the investment (time and money) you make on all your lead generation tactics.

- Conversion is one of the key leverage points in your business, one where you can make quick and instant gains for virtually zero increases in costs.

- A Conversion System is a set of logical steps from the moment a lead is generated to the moment a sale is made, with the goal being to generate as many good-quality sales as possible and at the right fee.

- On average, it takes seven positive contacts before a prospect says 'Yes'. Those that combine at least seven positive points of contact in their Conversion System will always gain more clients, customers or patients.

Creating a Conversion System

Step 1: Existing sales conversion optimisation.

Step 2: Map the stages of the Conversion System to create your Framework.

Step 3: Decide how many points of contact you require (minimum of seven, remember!).

Step 4: Write down the objective of each point of contact (two types of objectives: Courtesy Objectives and Next Step Objectives).

Step 5: Add Timeline.

Step 6: Decide the exact nature of each point of contact and create it.

Step 7: Add the Core Elements where you can.

Step 8: Keep following up to take advantage of 'The Moving Parade'.

Step 9: Monitor, test and improve.

THE MACHINE

CHAPTER 8

MAXIMISING CLIENT VALUE

In my last season at Leicester Tigers I picked up a very bad groin injury that required surgery. The professional term for the injury is 'Gilmore's Groin'. It was named after the surgeon who invented a type of surgery that fixed the problem. Until then, sportsmen and women who had the injury would have to retire. Basically, the constant changing of direction common amongst footballers, basketball players and rugby players would, with some people, result in one of the muscles around the groin area literally ripping clean apart. It was agony.

Prior to Gilmore, there was no way of stitching the muscle back together with long-lasting effect. Gilmore invented a special gauze and mesh-like material that he would attach to both ends of the torn muscle and, over a period of just six weeks, the fibres in the muscle would grow around the gauze creating a solid bond (well, that's what I was told!).

I had the surgery and, sure enough, after six weeks of rehab I was back to a level of fitness that enabled me to start full training.

Unfortunately, I couldn't fully regain my biggest attribute, my speed, and, at the top level of elite sport, just a 1% decrease can make all the difference. Truth was, I knew it was time to quit!

However, out of the blue I received a call from my agent Simon Cohen. He told me he'd been speaking to the owners of a club in the division below the Premiership who had significant investment and were looking to build a squad good enough to get promotion into the Premiership. They wanted a mix of young and experienced players. Simon told them I was considering retiring, but they asked if they could speak with me with the intention of persuading me to not hang my boots up just yet.

To cut a long story short, I knew I didn't have the speed to play at the highest level, but one league down would be fine. I passed my fitness test and began life for the first time in the Second Division.

At the time, I really was hell bent on retiring, but Moseley Rugby Club (based in Birmingham) offered me £45,000 a year for three years, part-time. It meant I could concentrate on building my business as I had done at Tigers and still get paid for doing what I loved.

I was going from a world-class club to (in my opinion) a second-rate club, all be it one with big ambitions. As it happens, in the 1970s Moseley were one of the biggest clubs in England,

and they wanted to bring back past glories. So, they did have a successful pedigree.

I had my reservations but, as with everything I do, I went into it fully committed. I did all the press and TV interviews prior to the first training session. Then we trained.

To be honest, I was pleasantly surprised with the quality of the training (the coach was Alan Lewis. He had coached Wales and knew what he was doing, although we never gelled). And on the plus side, my groin was feeling fine.

Then, after training we went back into the training rooms to shower. I turned the shower on and kept turning and turning the tap, but all that came out was a trickle. I went to the next shower ... and the next ... and the same thing. The showers were pathetic. I knew there and then that I'd made a mistake.

I should have retired.

You're probably wondering why I came to this conclusion on the basis of the showers not working. Well, here's my thought process ...

I'd been at a rugby club (Leicester Tigers) who put the players (their clients) at the heart of the club. Everything they did was with the players' development and welfare in mind. How they treated us, and our wives and partners, was world-class in every way.

When I turned on those showers at Moseley, I instantly knew I'd joined a club that didn't have that same philosophy. If they couldn't even spend the money (which wasn't a lot) to make sure the showers were working for their players, what else weren't they doing when it came to player development and welfare.

As it turned out, it was a disaster. My worst fears were realised at every turn. I joined in the August, and I was sacked in December, as they ran out of money and needed to cut their more expensive players.

So, what's the point of this story, I hear you ask?

Quite simply, you'll never create a world-class service business that maximises the sales and profit from its clients, customers or patients unless you focus on and treat your clients in a world-class way.

Figuratively speaking, even the little things such as the showers need to be world class. Otherwise, you won't retain your clients for long, and you won't ethically maximise your earnings from them.

It's simple ... don't have any 'broken showers' in your service business!

Broken showers are visible in many businesses. We've all experienced them before.

Therefore, this chapter focusses on making sure you don't have any 'broken showers' in your business and what to do to maximise income with your existing and all new clients, customers or patients.

To begin this crucial phase, you're going to use 'Moments of Truth' again. However, rather than using it to increase desire and adding points of contact to take the Perfect Client closer to the sale, you're going to use Moments of Truth to significantly increase 'Client Satisfaction', as well as ensure you don't have any 'broken showers' in your service business.

But before I go any further, let me take you through the process Jan Carlzon used with SAS airlines, because it will give you a really good understanding of how you can use Moments of Truth with clients and why it's so powerful ...

If you recall, the essence of Moments of Truth and why Carlzon created it was because SAS airlines were losing thousands of customers every week.

He was brought in to reverse this tide. The first thing he did shocked him. He went undercover, and over a period of a couple of weeks he pretended to be a prospect and a customer of SAS airlines.

Now remember, back in the early 1980s there was no internet and no mobile phones. So, to book a flight you had to use a landline. So, he rang SAS airlines to book his first flight. To his horror, the phone rang and rang and rang. After two minutes the phone was answered by a curt and unfriendly individual. After a prolonged and painful process Carlzon finally booked his ticket. He was travelling a couple of days later.

On the day of his flight he drove to the airport and found the SAS airlines check-in. Once again, he was shocked to see the kind of reception he received from the check-in staff. They too were rude and unfriendly. They didn't welcome him with a smile or upbeat greeting. They were going through the motions and looked like they'd much rather be somewhere else.

Then, when it came to baggage handling, he was dismayed when he saw there was no care and attention in terms of handling his baggage. The baggage handlers could be seen throwing his cases as if it was a competition to see who could fling them the furthest and inflict the greatest damage on them.

He was starting to see exactly why SAS were losing so many customers. But it didn't stop there ...

As he was boarding the plane, once again he noticed the staff were generally rude and uninviting, and although he was greeted with a smile as he entered the plane, the air stewards were again generally unhelpful and discourteous.

... and this type of 'service' continued thoughout the flight.

He was relieved when he arrived at his destination.

His experience was shocking. It was full of 'broken showers'. Every step of the way was littered with 'broken showers', and he knew he needed to act and act fast.

Now, this may seem a far-fetched story, but this is exactly what happened, and although I've used it to make a point to you, it does demonstrate what can happen if you don't put your clients, customers or patients first.

Carlzon now had first-hand experience of why SAS were losing thousands of customers every week.

And it was at this point when he created Moments of Truth. Let me tell you how he did it ...

He gathered all the heads of department and explained his experience with the airline. He detailed every point of contact and why it was so bad. He then told them that they needed a quick but long-lasting fix, otherwise the airline, would, within a matter of months, go bust.

So, he handed each of the heads of department a huge sheet of paper. He then told them to go back to their department and involve their staff and write down in chronological order all the points of contact they had within their departments with each customer. He explained that a point of contact was every interaction they had with a customer.

So, the heads of department went away and did what was asked of them. A few days later they came back to the boardroom with their completed sheets full of the points of contact each department had with their customers.

Carlzon was pleased. They'd really taken to the task and made sure each of their teams were part of the whole process.

He then asked each of the heads of department to read through all their points of contact and asked everyone else to comment positively and add any further points of contact they may had missed.

Carlzon then told them to go back to their teams and, for every point of contact with the customer, create a mini-system for that point of contact that would detail every step their staff would follow to ensure the experience the customer had at every point of contact raised their satisfaction level and made them feel special. He again reinforced the importance of getting their teams to take ownership and contribute to the entire process. The heads were to simply manage the process, while their staff were to come up with the ideas and create the mini systems at each point of contact.

After a week they all resumed in the boardroom. Each head detailed their mini systems for each point of contact, and again the rest of the heads would contribute to making each point of contact even better.

Carlzon was delighted with their progress. He then told them to go back to their teams, thank the staff and then implement everything within the month.

What happened next is legendary in the airline business. After implementing all the Moments of Truth in every department, SAS went from struggling to prosperous airline in six short months.

People raved about their customer service, raved about the wow moments the airline had created, and raved about how helpful, positive and friendly the staff were.

It was literally a complete transformation that cost only time, a little money and, of course, investment in training to ensure all team members could follow, to the letter, each of the mini systems within their departments.

Now, I appreciate that it's highly unlikely you run your business like SAS airlines did before Carlzon's intervention.

But what I want you to take away from this is the power of using Moments of Truth to create a service-led business that puts its clients, customers or patients at its heart.

A business that has no 'broken showers'.

Let's put this to work in your business, shall we?

Our Moments of Truth diagram shown in Figure 8.1 now has a slightly different look.

Notice that 'Desire' on the left axis has been replaced with Client Satisfaction.

Let me now share with you the process for implementing Moments of Truth into your service business ...

Write Down All Possible Points of Contact (Moments of Truth) You Have with Your Clients.

This is simple. Here's what you do ...

Use the 'Moments of Truth Design Table' (see Figure 8.2) and first identify every single interaction you have with your clients, customers or patients, then enter them in the 'Moment of Truth' column – every single one. Write these in chronological order (where possible).

Then, for each section, make sure you enter *when* the moment will happen and the details of *what* you'll be doing to make it a positive experience for the client, customer or patient.

Notice there are four sections.

<u>Section 1:</u> Client Acquired – Immediate Moments (in here, write down exactly what happens the moment you get a client).

For example ...

- 'Thank-You Email' sent
- 'Thank-You SMS' sent

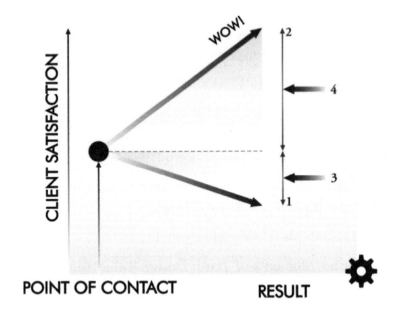

POINT OF CONTACT   **RESULT**

Legend:

1. The effect on the Perfect Client when the business doesn't actively focus on each interaction with them. Notice the Moment of Truth was a negative experience, reducing the Perfect Client's satisfaction and therefore creating discontent (no matter how small).
2. Moments of Truth approach. By breaking down each point of contact to ensure an excellent service-led experience, the satisfaction level is raised.
3. Shows the drop in client satisfaction when a business doesn't focus on each point of contact with its clients, customers or patients.
4. Shows the increase in Client Satisfaction gained by using Moments of Truth.

Figure 8.1. Moments of Truth to Create a Service-Led Organisation

MOMENT OF TRUTH	WHEN
CLIENT ACQUIRED – IMMEDIATE MOMENTS	
SERVICE DELIVERY MOMENTS	
ONGOING MOMENTS	
SPECIAL MOMENTS	
WORLD-CLASS CLIENT EXPERIENCE AND NO 'BROKEN SHOWERS'!	

Figure 8.2. Moments of Truth Design Table

Section 2: Service Delivery Moments (in here, write down the points of contact as you deliver your service to the client).

For example, if you're selling a business mentoring service ...

- Email meeting agenda (as per the Business Mentoring System).
- Send reminder SMS (as per the Business Mentoring System).
- Start the online meeting on time.
- Follow the Business Mentoring System to deliver a world-class meeting.

Section 3: Ongoing Moments (write down the things you're going to do to keep in touch with the client).

For example ...

- Send email mid-month, making sure the client is getting on with their tasks.

Section 4: Special Moments (write down things you're going to do that will WOW the client).

In the first three sections you've added only the basics, but they are still very important. This is the minimum level of positive interaction you should be having with your clients.

Without question, when you adopt Moments of Truth, you'll be adding so much more to each section. We do this with 'Special Moments of Truth'. For example, here's what I'd add:

Section 1 – Special Moments

What I'm going to reveal to you now will set you apart, not just from your competition, but from 99.9% of all businesses.

Once you get a new client, customer or patient after sending the 'Thank-You Email' and 'Thank-You SMS', you should mail them what I call a 'Welcome Pack' (see the images shown in Figure 8.3 as an example).

It's essential you send this by post (i.e. not digitally) to guarantee maximum effect.

What you do is get a mailing box designed in your branding with the name of your productised service on the front.

Believe me, when this is delivered, your clients will be astounded, and it reassures them that they've found a world-class provider.

Inside the box, add a letter welcoming them to your business and service and include any other elements that add to the value of it. For example ...

- Company-branded merchandise (as you can see, for our Sales Accelerator Programme [delivered by our coaches, mentors and consultants], we add two branded stress balls, the inference being that with our mentoring programme the client will suffer less from stress as they build their business).

- Video testimonials from clients on a memory stick (for example).

- Your book, or a book from an author that compliments your work (as you can see, we include my 'FORMULA' book).

- A copy of the latest issue of your newsletter.

Figure 8.3. The Welcome Pack

- And anything else you can think of that will make your new client think 'WOW!'

Believe me, this will create an amazing first impression of you and your mentoring programme. Don't think about doing it … just do it!

Section 2 – Special Moments

- Every time there is a significant result or milestone reached as part of delivering your service, send a 'Congratulations Gift'. The first gift could be a bottle of champagne! You'll be surprised how much difference this makes!

Section 3 – Special Moments

- Send your monthly printed newsletter.

This is NOT rocket science. We all instinctively know what will make people think 'WOW', because we're all customers of many other businesses. We can also count on one hand how many businesses we've bought from which make us think 'WOW'.

Another Great Example of Moments of Truth From an Unexpected Service-Based Industry

Just in case you have any doubts about the power of Moments of Truth and the effect it can have on your business, here's a great, unexpected example from a service-based industry – a cab (taxi) company (and … if they can do it, so can you!) …

Harvey Mackay (author of *Swim with the Sharks Without Being Eaten Alive*), tells a wonderful story about a cab driver that demonstrates Moments of Truth perfectly. It goes something like this ...

Harvey was waiting in line for a ride at the airport.

When a cab pulled up, the first thing Harvey noticed was that the taxi was polished to a bright shine.

Smartly dressed in a white shirt, black tie and freshly-pressed black slacks, the cab driver jumped out and rounded the car to open the back passenger door for Harvey.

He handed Harvey a laminated card and said:

'I'm Wally, your driver. While I'm loading your bags in the trunk, I'd like you to read my Mission Statement.'

Taken aback, Harvey read the card. It said: Wally's Mission Statement:

To get my customers to their destination in the quickest, safest and cheapest way possible in a friendly environment.

This blew Harvey away, especially when he noticed that the inside of the cab matched the outside: spotlessly clean!

As he slid behind the wheel, Wally said, 'Would you like a cup of coffee? I have a thermos of regular and one of decaf.'

Harvey said, jokingly, 'No, I'd prefer a soft drink.'

Wally smiled and said, 'No problem. I have a cooler up front with regular and Diet Coke, water and orange juice.'

Almost stuttering, Harvey said, 'I'll take a Diet Coke.'

Handing him his drink, Wally said, 'If you'd like something to read, I have the *Wall Street Journal*, *Time*, *Sports Illustrated* and *USA Today*.'

As they were pulling away, Wally handed Harvey another laminated card.

'These are the stations I get and the music they play if you'd like to listen to the radio.'

And, as if that were not enough, Wally told Harvey that he had the air conditioning on and asked if the temperature was comfortable for him.

Then he advised Harvey of the best route to his destination for that time of day.

He also let him know that he'd be happy to chat and tell him about some of the sights or, if Harvey preferred, to leave him with his own thoughts.

Then Harvey said, 'Tell me, Wally, have you always served customers like this?'

Wally smiled into the rear-view mirror. 'No, not always. In fact, it's only been in the last two years. For my first five years driving, I spent most of my time complaining like all the rest of the cabbies do.

'Then, I decided to do things differently. I looked around at the other cabs and their drivers. The cabs were dirty, the drivers were unfriendly, and the customers were unhappy. So, I decided to make some changes. I put in a few at a time. When my customers responded, well, I did more.'

'I take it that has paid off for you,' Harvey said.

'It sure has,' Wally replied. 'In my first year, I doubled my income from the previous year. This year I'll probably quadruple it. You were lucky to get me today. I don't sit at cabstands anymore.

'My customers call me for appointments on my cell phone or leave a message on my answering machine. If I can't pick them up myself, I get a reliable cabbie friend to do it, and I take a piece of the action.'

Wally was implementing Moments of Truth, even though he didn't realise it!

This true story shows if Moments of Truth can be so successful for a cab driver, it can work for YOU!

Using the Client Segmenting Matrix to Deliver the Right Support to the Right Clients

Okay, so you know that Moments of Truth are the foundation of making sure you keep clients for longer. This is fundamental to maximising client value.

But should you treat all clients the same?

No, you shouldn't.

Well, not if you want to maximise sales and profit from them, and your team to love what they're doing and at the same time think you're a wonderful boss!

To explain, let's return to the 'Client Segmenting Matrix' that you created back in Chapter 3. Figure 8.4 shows how it looks.

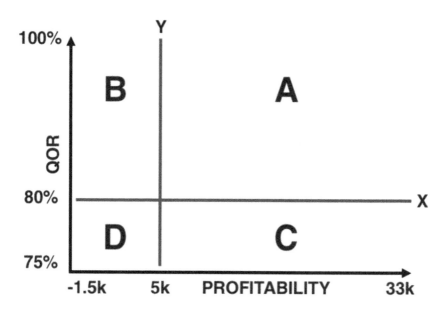

Figure 8.4. The Client Segmenting Matrix

Back in Chapter 3 we used the matrix to identify your Perfect Clients. If you recall they are located in segment A.

What I'm going to take you through now is a simple way to manage your entire client base and put in place a structure to service each segment to maximise sales and profits from them.

Right now your matrix has four segments. Let me explain how you should service them for maximum profit ...

SEGMENT A

As you know, these are your Perfect Clients. You have a great relationship with them, and they're profitable. Because of this, we often leave our best clients alone because they don't cause any trouble. They are a delight to work with, so we just let them 'get on with it'.

But this is a huge mistake.

By not focusing your attention on them, you really are missing out on extra sales and profits from them. Ideally, your A segment of clients should be given top priority and everyone in your business should know who every A client is, so they are treated like royalty.

You may even decide that you or other owners of the business take responsibility for them. Keep them close. Treat them well. Make them feel special. Do that, and you'll reap the rewards.

SEGMENT B

B clients are not as profitable as A clients, but you have a similar relationship with them. B clients are likely to be your 'bread and butter' clients. This will be your biggest segment, so they, of course, need attention, but ideally you should implement systems within the business to service them, rather than giving them personal attention. It's not sensible for the owners of the business to spend much time with B clients, because your team combined with systems will be able to keep them satisfied. I'll talk more about systemising the operational side of the business in Chapter 13.

SEGMENT C

C clients are your most challenging group. They are as profitable as A clients, but the relationship is poor. When they call the office or visit, everyone runs for cover! They cause huge stresses on the business in terms of time and attention, and none of your team enjoys working with them.

You don't want any C clients in your business, even though they are profitable. So how do you deal with them?

A solution is to meet with them to discuss their account. Then take them through the Client Segmenting Matrix. Draw it step by step and explain each of the segments. Then ask them where they think they fit!

I tell you now, having gone through this exercise dozens of times, they will almost certainly put themselves in the A segment.

Then, you show them exactly where they do fit and explain why they're a C client. Go into detail.

You'll get one of two reactions ...

They will either be horrified that you see them as a C client, and often this alone will change the way they interact with your business and your team. In effect, they quickly move up from C to A as a result. Or, they take offence and you agree to part ways.

Now, clearly because C clients are as profitable as A clients (in reality they're not because of the baggage they bring) strategically you need to have these conversations when you're in a position where to lose them wouldn't make a huge dent. And as long as you're following my advice in this book, you'll never be in a position to wonder where the next A client will come from. But, of course, proceed with caution and plan it in.

And you know what? It's weird how things work out, because almost every time you get rid of a C client, an A client is acquired almost immediately to replace them.

Also, don't underestimate the effect 'sacking' C clients will have on staff moral and how they think of you. Tell them that you're going to speak with your C clients and give them an ultimatum that they either improve the relationship or you will get rid of them. Even better, involve the team in the process of identifying C clients and put a plan in place to rid your business once and for all of C clients (they either move up to become an A client or they move out of the business entirely!).

SEGMENT D

D clients are by far your worse segment. They aren't profitable and the relationship you have with them is poor.

If that's the case, why have them in your business at all?

You have one option ...

Sack them.

Explain you've moved in a different direction and will no longer be able to work with them. My advice is to set up a relationship with a competitor and agree to sell them your D clients. Your D clients could be A clients to someone else, and why not profit from them by introducing them to another supplier who can handle them perfectly?

Figure 8.5 shows you exactly what's happening with your C and D clients in terms of the matrix. Your aim in terms of your client base is to have only clients in the upper section of the matrix, as shown in Figure 8.6.

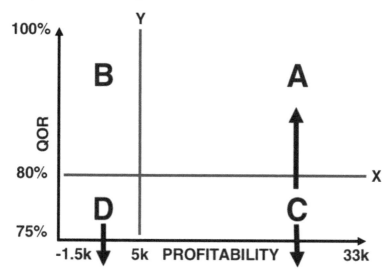

Figure 8.5. The Movement of Your C and D Clients

But we're not quite finished yet. You see, there is another 'hidden' and potentially highly profitable set of clients that you're going to identify.

These are what I call B+ clients.

They come from the B segment, but they are B clients who have the potential to become A clients.

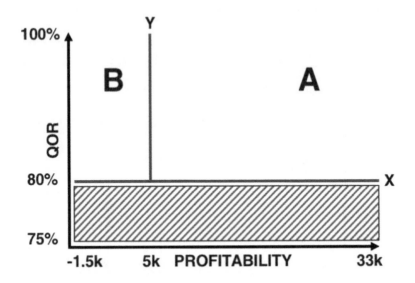

Figure 8.6. How Your Client Base Should Look

So, you should look through ALL your B clients and identify those clients who you believe in time and with more support from you and the team, could transition to become A clients.

There may even be a few B clients who right now could become A clients. Figure 8.7 shows how your matrix now looks.

To help B+ clients evolve into A clients, you should service them as you would B clients (by systems) but also give them more personal attention, like A clients. Now, they won't get the same level of service as A clients, but strategically you develop a nurturing-type approach that makes them feel special and helps put them on a path to becoming A clients.

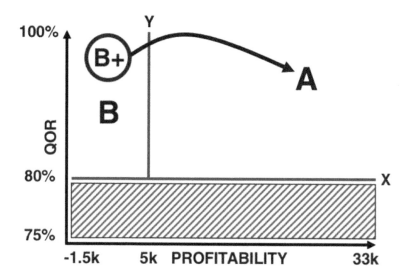

Figure 8.7. B+ Clients And Their Movement to Becoming a Client

Now you have the Perfect Client base being perfectly managed effectively by systems, by the team and by the owners of the business. This structure will ensure you retain clients for longer, generate many more referrals (see shortly), and that you'll be able to maximise the value of B, B+ and A clients.

The Four Sectors to Maximise Client Value

Okay, so we've ensured the client experience with you is amazing. We've also ensured you'll never have any 'broken showers'. We've also segmented your clients into five groups, with you striving to ultimately have only B, B+ and A clients in your business.

A superb foundation is now in place.

What you need to do next is capitalise on the relationship you're building with each client, customer or patient and to ethically maximise your sales and profits from them. This really is a weak area in most established service businesses, yet it's so easy to do.

There are four strategies for maximising client value ...

1. **Increase the frequency of purchase** (getting clients to buy more often).

2. **Increase referrals** (getting clients to recommend you more often).

3. **Increase average order value** (increasing the value of every sale).

4. **Reduce attrition** (keeping clients longer).

This is a very exciting part of building your service business. There are so many easy and highly profitable tactics you can add.

So, what I'm going to do now is to take you through the key tactics for each of the four areas, starting with 'Increasing the Frequency of Purchase' ...

Frequency of Purchase: Continuity in Advance

When I first started out in business, I would copy what other coaches and consultants at the time were doing. When it came to billing the client I would invoice them monthly, but only at the end of the month. So, for example, if I started working with a client on 1 September, I would send an invoice at the end of September for them to pay.

In almost every case, the payment wouldn't arrive for at least 2–4 weeks. Worse still, occasionally some clients wouldn't even pay. That meant I was working for FREE.

Operating your business this way is plain stupid. And I quickly learned that it's crazy to work before getting paid. Yet that's still how many service providers do it!

So, lesson number one is to never deliver your service *before being paid.*

Simply tell the new client, customer or patient how you work in terms of billing and that you bill in advance. Then there are no surprises. As soon as their full payment (or first payment) is made, you commence working together. Pretty simple!

Next, you should also try to build in 'continuity'.

If your service doesn't naturally lend itself to a recurring model (i.e. getting paid monthly, quarterly or annually) then try and find a way to deliver some or all of it so you can keep billing the client.

Adding a 'service contract' is a great way of doing this. Or it could be a quarterly 'check-up' or 'review' or 'analysis'. Think outside the box and figure out what you can keep selling to your clients, customers or patients, because, believe me, this will be the easiest sale you make!

Increase Referrals: The Referral System

As we discussed earlier when analysing why established service businesses stop growing, one of those factors is that many of them have grown the business mainly through referrals, but you can't then take the business to the next level just on referrals.

However, in my experience, most businesses have still only scratched the surface when it comes to referral generation.

That's because many people fail to ask for referrals from existing clients, customers or patients. They just hope and pray that their best clients refer others.

This 'passive' approach is not good enough.

You're 'hoping' that providing a world-class service will translate into goodwill, and that clients will refer others to you.

Of course, every good business gets referrals, but if I told you that with very little additional cost you could multiply the referrals you get by a factor of five or ten, would you be interested?

Well, that's exactly what will happen when you put in place an effective *referral system.*

Putting in place a referral system that focuses on getting referrals is one of the easiest and most rewarding things you can do.

How to Get More Referrals

The key to getting more referrals is to offer an *effective* incentive. This one thing puts your referral system on steroids and will multiply results. It doesn't have to be a cash incentive. Tickets to a sporting occasion, the opera, cinema, a donation to your client's favourite charity ... in fact, anything that the client values, is an excellent way of rewarding them. Remember, it doesn't cost you to acquire a referred client, so you can afford to give an incentive. Don't be tight! The bigger and more relevant the incentive, the more referrals you'll get. Fact!

Transform Your Service Business into a Referral 'Machine'

You'll find it relatively easy to put a referral system in place. Choose your incentive, communicate the referral system regularly, and you're on your way. Results will be good, but you can improve them significantly by immersing the business in the referral system.

Here's what I mean:

Your referral system will help to create a constant stream of referrals, but that's not good enough.

Sure, it will bring you many more new clients than ever before, but you can turbo-charge your referral system by INTEGRATING it completely into your service business. This is when you create your own 'Referral Mushroom', and your organisation transforms into a 'referral-based business'! The diagram in Figure 8.8 shows you exactly what I mean by this, and what you should do.

So, let's look at what you need to do to integrate a referral system completely into your business.

1. Add to all agendas

The last item on every meeting agenda with B, B+ and A clients should always be a reinforcement of your referral system.

When you get to this point in the agenda, reiterate to the client what your referral system involves (depending on the incentive you've chosen) and explain to them what they get as a result of a referral that converts into a client.

Tell them that your best clients are always referred ones, and that's why you invest so much time and effort in your referral programme.

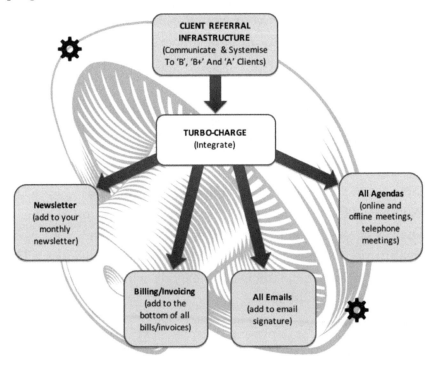

Figure 8.8. The Referral Mushroom

2. Add to all emails

Reinforce your key referral message in your email signature by adding your referral incentive.

266

3. Add to bills/invoices

Another great place to reinforce your referral system is at the bottom of all your bills/invoices.

4. Add to your monthly newsletter

Adding your referral message to the bottom of each page in your monthly printed newsletter (yes, it is still and always will be very effective to send a monthly newsletter!) is a great way to reinforce your referral programme.

In fact, your newsletter is an excellent place to add case studies from clients who have referred other people to you.

Increasing the Average Order Value: Up-Sell and Cross-Sell

Up-selling and cross-selling are two of the easiest yet most neglected tactics that can instantly add hundreds, thousands, even tens of thousands of pure profit to any service business.

Perhaps the best way to explain an up-sell is to use a well-known one that the food retailer McDonald's uses. Let's say you go into McDonald's and ask for any of their standard meals. The reply from the person serving you will be, 'Do you want to go large?' Basically, they are using a well-rehearsed 'Up-sell Statement' that makes it easy for the buyer to say 'yes' (they also now use this same approach with their 'self-order terminals', only the prompt is displayed rather than spoken).

With just six carefully-crafted words, McDonald's generates an up-sell that 30%–40% of customers say 'yes' to! Yes, that's another 30–40 people in every hundred that spend, say, a pound, dollar or euro more than they would have done had the Up-sell Statement not been used.

And just think for a moment ...

The cost to McDonald's for providing the larger-sized meal probably adds up to about 10p – so they've just created another 90p of profit on the sale with virtually no effort (six words).

To define up-sell more accurately:

An up-sell is when you move the client up to a larger quantity (bigger size, etc.) of the same service for a perceived preferential price.

Let me now explain cross-selling. Let's use the McDonald's example again to demonstrate how the cross-sell works.

You go into McDonald's and ask for any of their main dishes, such as a Big Mac or a Chicken Sandwich. The reply from the person serving you will be, 'Would you like fries with that?' Basically, they are using a well-rehearsed 'Cross-sell Statement' that makes it easy for the buyer to say 'yes'.

To define cross-sell more accurately:

A cross-sell is when you sell a complimentary product or service to the service initially bought.

So, why do the up-sell and cross-sell work so well?

The reason why they work so well is that the up-sell or cross-sell is used only after the person has made the decision to buy and become a client. That means they are comfortable with their decision. It's at this point they are much more susceptible to the up-sell or cross-sell, because they are in 'buying mode'.

You should be aiming to convert upwards of 30% of people with an up-sell or cross-sell.

Reducing Attrition: Delivering Results

World-class service businesses don't lose many clients. Unfortunately, we don't live in a perfect world, so you can't completely eliminate client attrition from your business, but much of what I've covered with you in this book will ensure you reduce client losses to a minimum. In fact, you almost certainly have clients that have been with you for many years already.

Without question, THE most important factor in retaining clients is *delivering results for them.*

It doesn't matter what type of service you sell, it solves a problem for your clients, customers or patients. As long as you consistently deliver that solution at a high level to your clients, then clients will keep coming back.

There are, of course, other elements to factor in, here, but if your primary focus is to achieve results for your clients and you succeed, you won't ever have an issue with customer attrition, and you'll retain 90% (or more) of your clients, customers or patients for many, many months, even years.

Let's take stock in terms of how far you've come ...

You've understood why established service businesses stop growing or aren't growing as fast as the owners would like, you've created the Perfect Client Avatar Profile, you've Productised Your Services, and you've created your Lead Generation, Conversion and Maximising Client Value systems. These things alone will have a major impact on your service business. But next, to get your business ready for accelerated growth and scaling, you first need to put these systems on autopilot, so they run 24/7. In the next chapter I'll explain exactly how you do that ...

Chapter Summary

- If you minimise 'broken showers' (in other words, treating your clients poorly) and implement Moments of Truth, your clients will love working with you and happily keep buying from you.

- Segmenting your client base using the 'Client Segmentation Matrix' ensures you can create a level of support that matches exactly where every client sits within your business.

- You should endeavour to eliminate (or move) C and D clients entirely from your business, to and create support systems combined with personal support from the business owners and the team to service B, B+ and A clients.

- Once the foundation of Moments of Truth and Client Segmentation are in place, you can successfully maximise client value.

- There are just four key areas to maximise client value:

  1. Increase the frequency of purchase.
  2. Increase referrals.
  3. Increase the average order value.
  4. Reduce attrition (client losses).

- Proven, low-cost tactics for maximising client value include:

  1. Continuity in Advance.
  2. Referral System.
  3. Up-sell and cross-sell.
  4. Deliver Results.

THE MACHINE

CHAPTER 9

PUTTING YOUR GROWTH ON AUTOPILOT

You may not have consciously realised it, but by creating sequential steps in the Lead Generation, Conversion and Maximising Client Value elements of THE MACHINE, you've created step-by-step SYSTEMS.

These three growth systems combine to ensure you ...

Generate a constant stream of leads, convert a high percentage of those leads into clients, customers or patients at the right fee, and then maximise the value of those clients, customers or patients.

But at the moment those systems are in effect all MANUAL systems. To get you ready for accelerating your growth and scaling up, we now need to automate as much of each system as we can.

In other words, you don't have a MACHINE yet.

The perfect machine is one that you turn on and it works almost entirely unattended ... relentlessly churning out results day after day.

It's quite simple ...

To create THE MACHINE for your service business we just need to automate ALL of the non-human steps of each system so they run on autopilot 24/7, 365 days a year.

Of course, this is a vital part of everything I'm asking you to do. Automation is KEY to creating THE MACHINE for your business.

There are a number of ways to do this, of course. I'm going to explain the best-practice ways for how we do it for our business and what we put in place for our clients so you too can have a fully automated growth system in place.

Here's exactly how to automate the non-human elements of your systems ...

Automating Your Lead Generation System

As you know, your Lead Generation System has four component steps ...

- STEP #1: The Crowd Puller

- STEP #2: Lead Capture Page

- STEP #3: The Media Circle

- STEP #4: Message to Market Tactics

So, let's look at how you make this system 100% fully automated ...

It actually starts with your 'Message to Market Ads'.

In other words, your lead generation campaigns.

You've identified the best Media Channels (ideally, you'll use all three) and the tactics within each of those Media Channels.

Let's address each Media Channel one at a time to show how you can 'piggyback' on their 'built-in automation' ...

E-Media

All the online advertising platforms (Google, YouTube, LinkedIn, Facebook, Instagram, and so on) give you the ability to drive Perfect Clients (targeted traffic) to your Lead Capture Page and to do it 24/7 (or at times you choose for your ads to run).

In effect, once you set up your campaigns, then the ad platform will automate the delivery of your ads to your Perfect Clients.

This is great. You're leveraging their automation tools without you having to think about it!

P-Media

When using P-Media, what the automation publishers provide is the delivery of your print ad every day, every week or every month within their publications. After testing, you'll simply let your ads run in each publication.

DM-Media

With DM-Media you have to take responsibility for automation. This is, however, relatively easy to do. After testing, you simply decide on the volume of direct mail you'll be sending to your Perfect Clients every month and ensure it happens, whether that's internally, or with a fulfilment house (someone who prints, packs and sends your direct mail on your behalf).

Lead Capture Page

As all three Media Channels, together with the tactics you use within them, are simply driving Perfect Clients to your Lead Capture Page(s), it doesn't matter what time of day anyone arrives on the page, because it's open 24/7.

The Opt-In

Once a Perfect Client lands on your Lead Capture Page they simply enter their details on your opt-in form.

So, as long as you've set up your Lead Generation System as I've described, you've already got automation in place.

That's a great start. Next your Conversion System kicks in, and here's the automation you need to put in place ...

Automating Your Conversion System

As soon as a Perfect Client enters their details into your opt-in form, it's important to integrate the form with an autoresponder. Autoresponders have been around since the internet was born in the early 1990s, so I'd be surprised if you weren't already taking advantage of them, but occasionally I still come across clients who aren't. Autoresponders are awesome, because they allow you to automate the first part of your Conversion System.

Popular stand-alone autoresponders include Mailchimp, Get Response and AWeber. But my advice, as you're already established, is to go a level up and invest in an online CRM system (customer relationship management). They act as autoresponders but will do much more. I personally recommend clients use Keap (formerly known as Infusionsoft). It's a truly awesome application, and it includes something known as 'automated processes', which few other CRM's do, yet it is crucial when it comes to automation (more on this later).

The autoresponder application you choose will provide you with a piece of code to enable you to integrate it with your Lead Capture Page, and your tech people will sort this within a couple of minutes for you.

This piece of code enables your Lead Capture Page and its form to 'talk' to your autoresponder, therefore allowing it to automatically push the data from your page into your autoresponder or CRM system.

That then enables you to set up an automated sequence of follow-up emails and SMS messages directly to the Perfect Client.

This, in turn, simply results in more sales!

Take a look at the follow-up sequence shown in Figure 9.1. This is the follow-up sequence for a client using a webinar as their Crowd Puller.

This follow-up sequence is more complicated than one you'd create for a Special Report or book, but it's a good example of what's possible when you use automation software.

We've built this in Keap, and if you take a look at Figure 9.2, this shows the sequence of emails behind one of the rectangular boxes ...

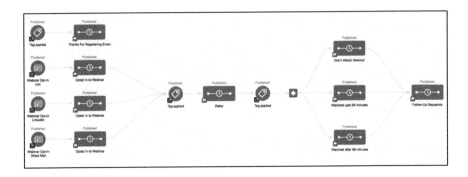

Figure 9.1. An Automated Follow-Up Sequence Built in Keap

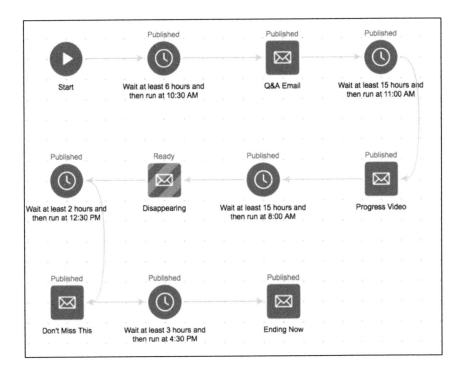

*Figure 9.2. The Steps Showing the Email Follow-Up Sequence
and the Timeframe for Sending Them*

Remember, all this happens automatically. You create the campaigns and sequences, write the email and SMS content, and let the software work its wonders by completely automating everything you put in place.

Crowd Pulling Synergy ...

Now, just pause for a minute.

I want you to imagine that you're a few months ahead ...

You've automated your Lead Generation System and your Conversion System, but instead of having just one Crowd Puller, you've got all three working in harmony.

As I've said, having ALL THREE Crowd Pullers in place will optimise your results. I referred to this back in Chapter 6 as 'Crowd Pulling Synergy'.

Here's why it works so well ...

Let's say you start with your Special Report. All your campaigns are driving Perfect Clients to opt-in. A number of them convert into clients but, of course, for several reasons (often timing), the majority don't.

But you've now also created your book and your webinar. So, in your follow-up sequences you then set up a series of emails first promoting your book and then promoting your webinar.

Now, everyone who initially registered for your Special Report and didn't convert into a client will first get your emails promoting your book, and then those that didn't become a client after that will get invited to your webinar.

Remember, all this is done automatically. You simply set up your system to deliver the sequence you want and let it run.

It doesn't matter what Crowd Puller you lead with, you then promote the other two to those people who were attracted to the first Crowd Puller. The diagram in Figure 9.3 shows how this looks ...

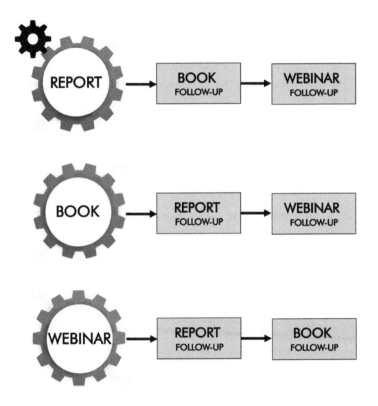

Figure 9.3. Crowd Pulling Synergy and Your Follow-Up Campaigns

You're delivering a preponderance of expertise first and, as a consequence, making it virtually impossible for people NOT to convert into clients, customers or patients.

This is the ULTIMATE client-generating system.

But so far, our Conversion System is using automation to deliver results right up to the follow-up sequencing.

What happens when you require human intervention? In other words, what happens when you have to call or meet with your prospective clients before they buy your services?

Well, you can automate EVERYTHING up to the meeting and everything beyond the meeting, but you can't automate the meeting or phone call itself, can you? But you can, of course, systemise the meeting and phone call so everyone in your organisation is following the best step-by-step approach to get the sale.

And this is where automated processes come to the fore ...

Automated processes don't stop at sending emails and SMS messages; they automate the completion of TASKS.

For example, let's say that after your meeting your Conversion System includes the following steps AFTER ...

- IMMEDIATE: Send 'Thank-You Email' to prospective client.
- NEXT DAY: Print and Mail 'Thank-You Pack' to prospective client.
- DAY 4: Call prospective client.

Note that I'm showing this for illustrative purposes and showing only three steps.

Now think of each step as a TASK within your business.

The tasks can't be fully automated, because, firstly, if the prospect becomes a client at the end of the meeting, then an onboarding sequence will begin (in other words, they must be excluded from the sequence of tasks above).

Secondly, each of the tasks involves at least one element of human intervention.

To ensure all these tasks are seamlessly completed by the right people and acted upon 100% of the time, we use automated processes.

In simple terms, automated processes instruct, at the right time, the people in your organisation whose role includes the fulfilment of the tasks outlined.

For example, if you carried out a meeting with a prospective client, let's say there are two outcomes.

Outcome one is that they become a client. Inside the system you'd then simply 'tag' the new client as a 'New Client', and then the automated processes would start the sequence of onboarding the client informing the relevant people in your business, what needed to be done and when.

If the prospective client doesn't convert at the meeting, you 'tag' them as 'Prospect Requires Follow-Up', and then the automated processes will kick in for the three steps I described above.

Hopefully, that makes sense.

You're using automated processes to bring order and automation to all the tasks required to be completed as part of your system. In this case your Conversion System.

And you'll use a combination of automation tools and automated processes to fulfil your Maximise Client Value system as well.

It doesn't matter what software you use; the point is that as long as it includes automated processes, you can automate much of your Conversion System once the data has been seamlessly transferred into it.

All you do is transfer your paper-based Conversion System (you should have already completed your Conversion System Framework Table) and transfer it to your software of choice.

The hard yards were done creating your Conversion System in the first place. You just transfer it into the software programme, and hey presto!

You've now got an automated Conversion System.

To explain this further, let's revert back to my completed Conversion System Framework Table in Chapter 7 (shown again in Figure 9.4).

Notice I've now filled in the timeline for each element.

This is what the automation will look like inside your CRM system ...

DAY	POINT OF CONTACT	OBJECTIVE
	LEAD GENERATED	
	STAGE 1: Expertise-Based Irresistible Offer	
0	Expertise-Based Irresistible Offer Video	
	Conversion Follow-Up Sequence	
	STAGE 2: Response Mechanics	
0	Receive in-bound form or call (or make out-bound call)	
	Partner speaks with prospect	
	STAGE 3: Meeting Arranged	
0	Email details of meeting	
1	Send confirmation letter	
3	Send Surprise Package	
	STAGE 4: Reception Greeting	
0	Receptionist greets prospect	
	Offer refreshments	
	Partner greets prospect	
	STAGE 5: The Meeting	
0	Follow meeting sales process	
	Ask for the order	
	STAGE 6: Post Meeting	
0	Meeting follow-up letter	
3	Follow-up phone call	
5+	Follow-up system	
	SALE & NEW CLIENT ACQUIRED	
	MAXIMISING CLIENT VALUE SYSTEM	

Figure 9.4. The Conversion System Framework Table

STAGE 1: Expertise-Based Irresistible Offer

- Once the details are entered into the opt-in form, the visitor is redirected to the Expertise-Based Irresistible Offer page, which includes a video of one of the partners explaining how your expertise and services can help.

  They encourage the prospect to complete the application and then schedule a meeting.

  Prior to booking a meeting, the prospect has a couple of questions, so they first call the office.

STAGE 2: Response Mechanics

- The call comes into the office. The people answering the phones have an optimised call answering script, which is pre-loaded into the CRM system for them to read (the reality is that you get the staff answering the phones to learn the script so it sounds natural, but it's still there for reference inside the CRM system).

  A new contact record was created when they completed the opt-in form, but now additional details, such as the name of the business and other data, is entered into the record for this lead.

- The lead is then passed on to an available partner who uses the qualification questionnaire (loaded as a form inside the CRM system) to determine the quality of the lead and to arrange a meeting.

STAGE 3: Meeting Arranged

- Once the meeting has been arranged and the call ended, the partner presses the complete button on the form, which automatically triggers the next sequence of events.

- The email confirming the meeting is merged with the relevant data entered into the form (such as the first name of the lead, the date and time of the meeting, and so on) and sent 15 minutes later.

- One day later, the confirmation letter is triggered by the CRM system and automatically merged, and the secretary prints it out on the company's letterhead, inserts it into a window envelope, affixes a stamp and then adds it to the mail pile for the post office later that day.

- Three days later, the Surprise Package cover letter is triggered by the system as above. The secretary adds the additional information to make up the package, inserts it into a large brown envelope and places it on the mail pile.

STAGE 4: Reception Greeting

- Each morning the CRM system shows which leads are coming to the office for a meeting and at what time. The reception area is primed and staged as per the instructions detailed in the CRM system. The partner reviews the contact's details stored in the CRM ready for the meeting.

- The receptionist greets each person by name (detailed in the CRM system) and offers them a drink from the drinks menu. They note their favoured drink on the form and later enter those details in the form ready for the next time the lead (or hopefully client) returns to the office.

- The partner is informed automatically by the system, once the drink details have been entered, that the prospect is in reception.

- The partner waits a couple of minutes and then greets the prospect.

STAGE 5: The Meeting

- The meeting room has already been 'staged' by the receptionist as per the instructions in the CRM system. That includes making sure the flip chart has paper, that the computer is set up for television and ready for presentation, that the speakers are working for video, etc.

- The partner then follows the 'Meeting Sales Process', as detailed in the CRM system. Obviously, the partner will have learned this system and won't be referring to the CRM system during the meeting.

- At the end of the meeting, the partner asks for the order.

STAGE 6: Post-Meeting

- Assuming the prospect didn't convert into a client at the meeting, the partner enters the additional details gained during the meeting into the 'Meeting Form' in the CRM system, and once the 'enter' button is clicked, the CRM system takes over. It merges and prints the 'Meeting Follow-Up Letter', ready for the receptionist to mail.

- Three days later the CRM system alerts the partner to make the follow-up call. The partner uses the script in the CRM system.

- If the prospect hasn't converted into a client at this stage, the CRM system then fulfils the follow-up sequence already entered into it.

- Once the prospect converts into a client, the receptionist opens their contact record, changes them from lead to client, and then the 'Customer Maximisation System' takes over, again automated by the CRM system.

As you can see, what we've done is automate the Conversion System using your CRM software. Once you've completed your Conversion System Framework Table, it's just a case of transferring your hard copy into your CRM system, and then you're on your way.

Beautiful!

Automating Your Maximising Client Value System

You've now successfully automated your Lead Generation and Conversion Systems. All that's left is to automate the final piece of the jigsaw (and arguably the most important).

As soon as you acquire a client you need to automate the Moments of Truth steps you've already completed, and then automate the tactics and strategies you're using to maximise client value.

Once again, you're going to use your CRM system to do this, just like you've done with your Conversion System.

Firstly, you're going to transfer the hard copy details from your Moments of Truth Design Table to your CRM system.

You're then going to add the additional maximising client value tactics to it to ensure you maximise the earning potential from every client, customer or patient.

For example, if you've created various up-sell and cross-sell scripts, these will also be in the CRM system, and staff will have been trained on them so that at the point of purchase the scripts are delivered to the client to maximise the value and profit of the sale.

As mentioned above, once the lead converts into a client, customer or patient, their contact record in the CRM is changed from 'lead' to client', which then triggers the sequence.

I appreciate we've jumped into the realms of technology now, and if you're anything like me, you don't find these things easy.

Even if you do, my recommendation is to find people who have this expertise and pay them to set them up for you.

They can either be brought on as a member of your team or as a supplier, but either way, they will save you a huge amount of time, frustration and money ... as long as they have the required level of knowledge.

Conclusion

Very few service businesses, even established service businesses, have systemised and automated their growth like I've just shown you.

It doesn't matter what type of service you sell. Whether it's online or offline, or bricks and mortar, this is a proven model that works time and time again. Once you automate, it frees you up to start doing the things you want to do in your business and in your life!

... and, best of all ...

It enables you to further ACCELERATE the growth of your business and SCALE UP!

And that's what we'll focus on in the next few chapters.

Chapter Summary

- You must automate your Lead Generation, Conversion and Maximising Client Value systems to further accelerate the growth of your business.

- Automation reduces your dependence on people, frees up a huge amount of your time, reduces mistakes and enhances results. More importantly, it gets the business in prime position to start scaling.

- You'll use a CRM system that includes automated processes to automate your three systems.

CHAPTER 10

THE SCALING-UP PARAMETERS

You've now built most of THE MACHINE and implemented it into your service business. Congratulations! Don't underestimate what you've achieved. You've come a long way. However, the last piece of the jigsaw is the most important. With the foundation firmly in place, you can now scale your business and take it to the next level and beyond.

To do that, we need to apply something I call the 'Scaling-Up Parameters'.

These are the strategies you'll apply to ensure you scale without the added burden that growth brings to every organisation. They are all crucial and work in tandem with one another to make scaling up as seamless and as painless as absolutely possible. As you're already running an established business, it's likely you'll have already gone through some kind of scaling up. It's got you to where you are today. But now it's time to push on, and when you apply the Scaling-Up Parameters, your MACHINE is going to deliver exactly what you want in terms of growth, AND make your business more valuable if and when you decide to exit.

There are five Scaling-Up Parameters:

1. Pump THE MACHINE with Channels and Tactics.

2. Applying the Science of Marginal Gains.

3. Systems, Systems, Systems.

4. Staffing the Expansion.

5. The Perfect Scaling-Up Model.

I'll take you through each one over the next five chapters ...

CHAPTER 11

PUMP THE MACHINE WITH CHANNELS AND TACTICS

I mentioned back in Chapter 6 about the worst number in business being 'one'. I also said that it's prudent to launch only one Lead Generation campaign at a time.

It's therefore time to start using the virtues of the Media Circle, and to launch multiple channels and tactics to scale up your lead generation, therefore scaling up the number of clients, customers and patients you acquire.

This is the easiest way to scale your business, but it must be based around sound principles. My advice is for you to still add only one tactic at a time, and, once it's working well for you, then add another, and so on.

You lose nothing by being prudent and cautious.

Ultimately, as you scale with channels and tactics, you'll have a very powerful Lead Generation strategy in place that will look like the diagram in Figure 11.1.

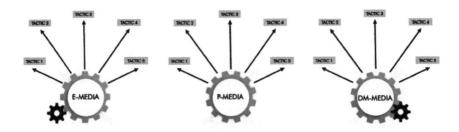

Figure 11.1. Scaling with media Channels and Tactics

Before I explain how you can put the same model in place, I want to take this opportunity to give you a set of rules or guiding principles, if you like, in terms of what you should be doing when it comes to your Lead Generation campaigns, because if you're not careful, it's easy to lose the shirt off your back, especially with online advertising.

These rules are important, because they will help you form your strategy when it comes to 'investing' in your Lead Generation campaigns.

Unfortunately, you can't escape the fact that scaling up does require you to invest in Lead Generation.

It's the fuel that feeds your entire MACHINE.

But over the years I've developed a set of rules that we use in our business and in our clients' businesses to ensure scaling up with channels and tactics can be done highly effectively with minimal risk and maximum return.

Let me take you through each one ...

RULE #1: Your Perfect Client ALWAYS Comes First

Don't ever be lured by the bright lights of the next new amazing social media platform. Remember, you choose the channels and tactics that you know with absolute certainty can help you reach your Perfect Clients.

That is your guiding principle. Don't ever veer away from that. Do your research. If your Perfect Clients can be reached by a specific tactic, then you should absolutely test it (see Rule #4), but if not, leave well alone. Believe me, this first rule will save you a lot of time and money! Don't break it.

RULE #2: Focus on Cost of Acquisition and Lifetime Customer Value, NOT on Cost Per Lead

There's so much hype around the cost to generate a lead. Many of the 'gurus' talk about using the likes of YouTube or Facebook to achieve a low cost per lead. But that's not where your focus should lie. Remember, your guiding principle is to use only a tactic where you know your Perfect Clients can be reached.

And once you do that, then your focus should be on the cost of acquisition and Lifetime Customer Value, NOT on cost per lead.

You see, you could have a campaign on Facebook that's delivering you leads at just £10 or £15, but if none of them convert, then it's a waste. Or if it takes 250 leads at a cost of £15 a lead, to get a sale, your cost of acquisition is £3750. Now that might be awesome for you (profitable), or terrible (loss making), but the point I'm trying to make is you must base your financial analysis on the cost of acquisition and then Lifetime Customer Value.

When you make this transition from cost per lead to cost of acquisition and Lifetime Customer Value, it is a seismic shift and will enable you to grow and scale faster than you ever thought possible.

Cost of acquisition is simply the cost of acquiring a client. For example, if you spend £500 on a Google Ads campaign, and it generates you two clients, then your cost of acquisition is £250 (£500 divided by two clients).

Lifetime Customer Value is the profit a client generates over the lifetime of their relationship with you. This number will be an average across your client base. For example, if, on average, clients keep buying from you for three years and, on average, the gross profit per year is £2000, then your Lifetime Customer Value is £6000.

My advice with Lifetime Customer Value is to have three numbers: one for A clients, one for B clients and one for B+ clients. Then create your average across all three. That way, it gives you a clear understanding of how much, on average, each segment of your client base is worth (you did this exercise earlier), which you'll find especially useful.

Once you've done that, you can take a 100% strategic approach to your lead generation rather than guessing and hoping.

Let me explain the rationale to go through …

Let's say you launch a LinkedIn ads campaign. You let it run for two weeks. During this time you spend £1500.

The good news is that you acquired two clients.

So your cost of acquisition is £750.

Your service is sold at £2000 and your gross margin is 70%. Therefore, on this first transaction you make a profit of £650 per sale (£2000 × 70% = £1400 − £750 = £650). But your Lifetime Customer Value is £6000, so over the lifetime of the relationship you're making on average £5250 (£6000 − £750).

Make sense?

If this scenario plays out, you know that it makes good sense to continue with LinkedIn, because it's delivering profitable clients for you, even from the first sale.

But let's say the above numbers still apply but instead of your service selling for £2000, it instead sells for £600.

Your Lifetime Customer Value is the same, which means on the first sale you make a loss of £150, but over the lifetime of the relationship you're still making £5250 (£6000 − £750).

If this scenario plays out, you have an initial challenge in terms of cash flow, but as long as you can get into profit quickly (by selling more to the client as soon as you can) then you alleviate the problem quickly, and you can get into positive cash flow.

In my opinion, this scenario is still a great one to have, because you know you're still going to make £5250 over the lifetime of that client. You just have to make sure you cover the initial losses.

The real challenge comes when either the cost to acquire the client or your Lifetime Customer Value means there's little margin and profit to play with. If that's the case, you have two options …

Option 1: Cut your losses and ditch the tactic, or …

Option 2: Use Scaling-Up Parameter 2 – Marginal Gains. You will be staggered at how much you can improve your cost of acquisition and Lifetime Customer Value when you apply Marginal Gains across your service business. Make the changes and test again. See what effect it has on the numbers, and then either apply Marginal Gains again to improve your numbers further or cut your losses.

My advice ultimately is for you to decide on what your 'This Works For Me Number' is going to be.

This number is the cost of acquisition amount that you set that means if it's less than this you keep moving forward with that tactic and campaign. If it's over this amount, you stop and put it down to learning.

RULE #3: Accept There Will Be Wastage

Perhaps one of the most important realities you must come to terms with, especially if you haven't spent much previously on campaigns, is that you will waste some money at the beginning of each campaign.

As long as you apply Rule #4, then you'll keep your losses to a minimum, but you will be doing a lot of testing. If you're using E-Media, then you'll be testing your online ads. Some won't work, some will deliver okay results and some will hopefully deliver excellent results.

The same goes when you're using P-Media and DM-Media. As you'll see when we discuss Marginal Gains, testing your campaigns is one of the big leverage points, but just remember some campaigns and tactics won't work.

You learn a lot from your campaign failures, but this is the real world, and you have to accept that not everything is going to work and go to plan, even when you follow everything in this book. That's the reality of campaign management. But as long as you do test, then you will get more than enough 'winners' to off-set some of your losses.

It's best I tell you this now, so you can prepare yourself. Just accept wastage as part of the process.

RULE #4: Always Use the Minimum Risk Formula

Before I introduce the Minimum Risk Formula, let me tell you another story ...

While I was playing for Leicester Tigers, I set up another business with a fellow player. Matt Poole played in the second row alongside Martin Johnson (England's World Cup–winning captain).

He, like me, was very entrepreneurial, and 1997 was an exceptional year of sporting success for the city of Leicester.

Tigers won the domestic cup (the Pilkington Cup), Leicester City F.C. won the League Cup, Leicestershire County Cricket Club won the County Championship and Martin Johnson was picked to captain the British and Irish Lions in South Africa in the summer.

It was an unprecedented and never-to-be-repeated season for the three big Leicester clubs.

But no one was doing anything to celebrate this success. So, Matt and I created a company called Top Table Corporate Events

Limited, and our first event would be a dinner to celebrate Leicester's astonishing sporting success in 1997.

We called the dinner 'The Captains Celebration Dinner'. Figure 11.2 shows the brochure we used to sell tickets.

We then approached each of the clubs and asked them all if they would happily give us the contact details of all their corporate sponsors, box holders and advertisers, and to our surprise, they all agreed (that just wouldn't happen now, because of data protection).

In other words, we had a list of Perfect Clients.

We had the contact details of every business that was supporting each club.

In all, we had just under 10,000 business contacts ... each and every one of them an avid sporting investor and fan.

We put the whole evening together, which would be held in Leicester City's new multi-million pound stand in the 'Carling Belvoir Suite'. Tickets were £49.95 each, and there were 300 tickets available.

I created a simple mailing piece (shown in Figure 5.26), and we mailed the entire list. We sold out within three days. The sponsorship money we received from the five major sponsors paid for the mailing and the cost of the food, etc.

Figure 11.2. The Captains Celebration Dinner Brochure

Figure 11.3. The Captains Celebration Dinner Brochure

Just in ticket sales we generated £14,985, which was effectively our profit from the evening.

It was a major success, but what happened next put the company out of business (there are two important lessons) ...

Following the success of the Captains Dinner, Matt and I created the Leicestershire Sporting Luncheon Club. We figured that on the back of the success of the dinner and the fact that outside London, Leicester was the sporting capital of the UK at the time, there was a real desire to have a sporting luncheon club.

Matt and I were so excited.

I wrote a two-page sales letter, and we both 'fell in love with it', so much so that we decided to mail the entire list of 10,000 that we had acquired from all the clubs.

That mailing cost just over £15,000 to print and mail. That was basically all our profit from the Captain's Dinner. Having written the letter, fallen in love with it and anticipating 150 members joining the club at £349 per year (£297 for the lunches and £50 per year membership fee), it would be a decent business right from the outset, especially when adding sponsorship monies.

It simply couldn't fail ... so, as I said we sent the mailing pack out in April 1998. You can see an example of the letter in Figure 11.4.

Then we waited (if you've ever used direct mail, you'll know the wait between sending the mailing piece out and getting the first responses is agonising).

TOP TABLE

Corporate Events Limited

The Cottage, Keyham

Introducing Leicester's only Sporting Luncheon Club

Membership is restricted to 150 places... So hurry if you don't want to miss out!

Dear Fellow Sports Enthusiast

I'll get straight to the point. We live in a city that thrives on its sporting prowess. In fact we're sporting "nuts." That's why we've started Leicester's **only** Sporting Luncheon Club. It's for busy <u>business people</u> like you who enjoy sport and like mixing with people who have similar fervent sporting interests. But it's like no other Sporting Luncheon Club...

First and foremost it's a <u>Member's Club</u>. Once we reach 150 Members our doors will close. No other Memberships will be on offer. You'll be part of a very exclusive Sporting Club. Jealousy will be rife amongst your friends and business colleagues.

Of course being a member of such a prestigious Club has many other benefits. You'll receive...

• **Ten exquisite 3 course lunches** throughout the year at Leicester City's Gary Lineker Suite. You only pay for your drinks. There are no hidden extras!

• **Hilarious sporting guest speakers** at every luncheon. We've hand picked the first three - Geoff Miller, Brian Voyle-Morgan and Gareth Chilcott. Each one is accompanied by the brilliant compere Dave Ismay. However, as it's your Club we're giving you the opportunity to choose the next seven guest speakers from our specially selected group of sought after speakers.

• **A limited edition print** of only 200 copies - by Leicester's No.1 sporting artist - Tony Booker. Framed and signed by the three title winning Leicester captains - Steve Walsh, Martin Johnson and James Whitaker - your personalised print will be branded to your specification with, for example, your name and company name. <u>This alone is worth at least £150.00.</u>

• **A free copy of the best selling golf video** "The Swing - A lesson for Life" by John Cook and Mark Wallace - two of Europe's finest golf coaches, <u>worth £12.99</u>.

• **Excellent networking opportunities** with other members. We aim to compile an index of all the Members' products and services to encourage business interaction. <u>You'll easily pay for your membership with business generated from the relationships you forge with other members.</u>

Please read on

Figure 11.4. Sporting Luncheon Club Sales Letter

• **Member's discount scheme.** Exclusively for Members, a discount scheme for goods by Rolex, Adidas, Sony, Panasonic, Philips, Canon, LG, Kenwood, Cartier and many others. These will be available to you - and your friends and family - at prices well below those on the High Street. Just one call to our special ordering point will enable you to claim these special discounts. Another opportunity to save the price of your membership!

• **Practical Golf tips.** John Cook our golf adviser will be on hand at every lunch to provide you with practical golf tips. John is a four times European Tour winner and official PGA Coach to the Golf Union and a number of European Tour players.

• **Your very own exclusive member's tie** - wear it with pride.

• **Your membership is fully transferable.** If you can't make a date, treat someone else! Of course if you have more than one Membership you have the added bonus of inviting any client, prospect, colleague or friend to come along with you. This flexibility is very important - we want your membership of the Sporting Luncheon Club to be another source of income for your business!

You get all these benefits and ten lunches for only £299 plus £50 membership (renewable every year).

So, how do you join this exclusive Sporting Luncheon Club? All you have to do is fill in and return the tear-off slip enclosed. You can then fax it to us on **0116 251 5510**, or place it in the envelope provided (no stamp required). Quicker still, confirm your Membership by calling us direct on **0116 253 0920**. Hurry if you don't want to miss out.

Your 'Better Than Risk Free' Guarantee. Membership to the Luncheon Club has a 'better than risk free' guarantee. If after the first lunch you're in any way dissatisfied with any aspect of the Luncheon Club, I'll refund all your money - no quibble. Furthermore, you can keep the free golf video worth £12.99. So at worst you'll have had a free lunch, listened to Geoff Miller and received a free video worth £12.99 - I can't be fairer than that!

So don't delay. Don't put this letter down and say to yourself "yeah, this sounds great, I'll get in touch in the next couple of days." Do it now or you could miss out. I don't want to have to say to you "Sorry, we're full up!"

Thanks for your time.

Regards

Steve Hackney

NB. The first lunch is on Friday May 21st. 'Phone us now on 0116 253 0920 or fax us on 0116 251 5510 to reserve your membership. Don't forget membership is restricted to 150 and also remember that if after the first lunch you're not totally satisfied, we'll refund all your money, and you can keep the free golf video worth £12.99. There really is nothing to lose!

Figure 11.4. Sporting Luncheon Club Sales Letter

Then three days later we got our first order … and the second … and the third.

Then on the fourth day we got two more orders.

Then guess what happened?

That was it. We didn't receive another order. Not one more.

Our amazing sporting luncheon club had a grand total of five members.

It was a complete disaster.

And, as we'd wasted all £15,000 of profit in the business on that one mailing, Matt and I decided to call it quits and close the business.

So, why tell you this story now?

Well, as I explained, there are two very important lessons to be learned from it that are as relevant today as they were back in 1998.

Firstly, don't ever 'fall in love' with your campaigns. This is a very dangerous thing to do, because, as it did with Matt and I, it lulls you into a false sense of security. What *you* think of your campaign is absolutely irrelevant. Let your Perfect Clients tell you how good it is from the number of leads and clients you generate! That's the acid test, _not_ what you think about it!

Secondly, no matter how good you think your campaigns are … no matter how good you think your service is … no matter how unique your service is (and it will be having applied what you're learning I this book) … you must **TEST SMALL**.

Think about it ...

If Matt and I had first sent a test mailing to, say, a thousand people on the list, that would have cost us around £1500, but the results would have told us a huge amount about the campaign and the luncheon club concept. That test mailing would have produced one or two members at most, so it would have forced us to change the offer or maybe even ditch the concept completely, but we'd still have about £13,000 left in profits, and you could do a lot with that kind of money back in 1998!

As a result of this experience, I vowed I'd never risk everything ever again, no matter how good the campaign and the product or service was.

I would test small.

I would use what I have come to call the 'Minimum Risk Formula'.

In other words, I would spend as little as I could to give me a statistically valid result, and, based on results, that would then determine the next steps.

If the test went well, I would then gradually increase the budget each time, so I would never unnecessarily financially expose myself. If the test went badly, I would re-evaluate (ditch or test again) ... and so on.

You lose nothing using the Minimum Risk Formula.

If your first test works well, it's highly likely your second test will work well too, and so on. If your first test doesn't work well, it's highly likely that if you don't change anything, your second and third tests will fail, too.

So, the moral of the story is twofold ... don't ever fall in love with your campaigns, and ALWAYS use the Minimum Risk Formula to test small.

That way, you are never going to expose yourself financially.

*****

If you follow these four rules, you can start adding channels and tactics and build up your campaigns. As I said, adding channels and tactics is going to give you the leverage and scale you desire, and it's a process we obviously work hard to achieve with all our clients.

The reality is, you have to add channels and tactics to take your service business to the next level, but the next Scaling- Up Parameter will add rocket fuel ...

Chapter Summary

- To scale up you must start adding additional Media Channels and tactics to drive your Lead Generation System.

- Once you're finished, you will ideally have campaigns running across all three Media Channels and multiple tactics.

- Don't add multiple tactics all at once. Add one at a time.

- There are four simple rules to follow when adding Media Channels and tactics ...

    1. RULE #1: Your Perfect Client ALWAYS Comes First.

    2. RULE #2: Focus on Cost of Acquisition and Lifetime Customer Value, NOT on Cost Per Lead.

    3. RULE #3: Accept There Will Be Wastage.

    4. RULE #4: Always Use the Minimum Risk Formula.

THE MACHINE

CHAPTER 12

APPLYING THE SCIENCE OF MARGINAL GAINS

This second Scaling-Up Parameter will revolutionise your service business if you immerse yourself, your team and the whole business in it.

I'm going to take you through the Science of Marginal Gains', which is the compounding effect of improving tiny elements of your business which, when combined, produce significantly better results.

Marginal gains was popularised by Sir David Brailsford. He used the process of Marginal Gains when he was the performance director of British Cycling and created one of the most successful teams in the history of Olympic sport.

He attributed that success to the work that he and his coaches and athletes did with regard to applying Marginal Gains across the entire breadth of performance. That included the athlete, the bikes themselves and the support team around each athlete.

And they broke every facet down into hundreds of different elements and sought to improve every one by 1%.

That may seem a tiny amount ... but, if you think about it, over hundreds and hundreds of different elements, those tiny improvements soon mount up, and the compounding effect results in huge increases in performance over time ... and it's exactly the same with your service business.

Let me explain how this looks from a scientific perspective ...

For this first formula shown in Figure 12.1, the number says, 1.01 to the power of 365 ...

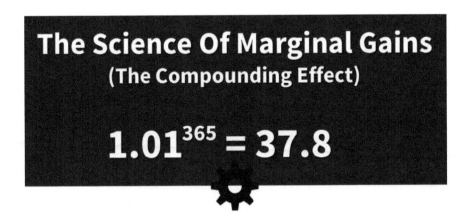

Figure 12.1: Marginal Gains Formula 1

Applying The Science Of Marginal Gains

What that basically means is that you're improving results and performance by 1% every day, over 365 days. That's just 1%.

The compounding effect of that, is giving you almost 38 times the result compared to where you started from.

That's 3800%.

Just pause for a second and digest what I've just told you. Improving the performance of your service business by just 1% every day for 365 days gives you a compound result of 38 times from where you started.

Imagine applying that across your business. But let's say the improvement was just half of one percent, the results are still going to be significant.

Now, the downside of the compounding effect of Marginal Gains is this ... if you're not improving, then you're going backwards.

If you're going backwards by only 1% a day, you can actually see that over a 365-day period, the compounding effect gives you a downturn, if you like. Figure 12.2 shows you how this looks.

As you can see, you go from 0.99 to 0.03. That's a significant reduction in the growth of the business; in fact, it's shrinking very quickly.

And the third formula shown in Figure 12.3 shows the compound effect of improving just 30 steps in your Lead Generation, Conversion and Maximising Client Value systems by 5%. That will result in an astonishing 400% improvement in results.

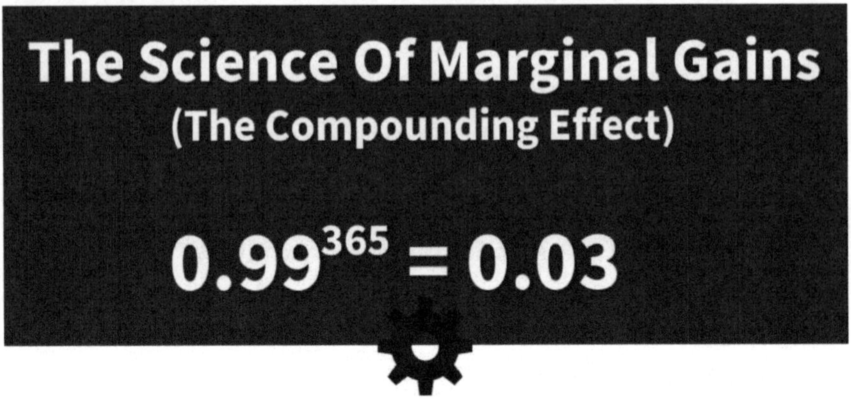

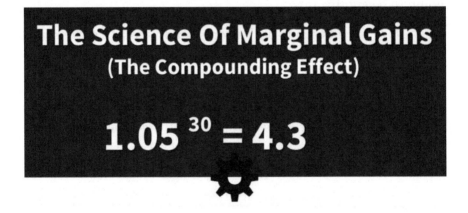

The Science Of Marginal Gains
(The Compounding Effect)

$$0.99^{365} = 0.03$$

Figure 12.2: Marginal Gains Formula 2

The Science Of Marginal Gains
(The Compounding Effect)

$$1.05^{30} = 4.3$$

Figure 12.3: Marginal Gains Formula 3

This is a really vivid way of looking at the Science of Marginal Gains and the compounding effect that you can obtain by tweaking things just by a small percentage on everything that you do. That's the approach that I talk about when growing any service business or improving elements of it like your MACHINE.

As long as you have a philosophy of Marginal Gains and you apply it across your business, then *multiplying* your results isn't such a far-fetched thing.

I've seen it with my businesses, and I've seen it with all our clients' businesses.

The concept of Marginal Gains really is a very, very powerful approach, so let me show you how to apply it to your own business.

The good news is that having taken you this far into THE MACHINE, I've already given you the roadmap and an easy way to apply Marginal Gains.

At the high level, you can apply Marginal Gains to …

- Your Perfect Client Avatar: Have you really laser-beam focused on your Perfect Clients? Scrutinise what you've already done. Be brutal in your assessment. What else can you squeeze out that will bring you closer to perfection.

- Productise Your Services: Is your 'product' illustration easy to understand? Does it convey expertise? Have you followed the 'STT Triangle' to the letter?

- Lead Generation System: Take every step and break it down. Are you using all the appropriate Core Elements? What can you do to improve and optimise them (test your landing pages, test your headlines, test the title and hero shot of your Crowd Puller, and so on)?

- Conversion System: Again, look at every step you've put in place and scrutinise it. Can you add more steps, or have you got too many? Are you applying all the relevant Core Elements? What can you do to optimise them? Can you apply more Moments of Truth? Can you add more WOW! Moments?

- Maximising Client Value System: What can you do to improve your onboarding system? Can you add more Moments of Truth? What other WOW! Moments can you add?

- Automate: Have you automated all the non-human elements of your three systems? Can you improve the automation?

Across THE MACHINE, you'll have dozens and dozens of elements that you can apply Marginal Gains to.

My advice is to create a checklist of Marginal Gains for every component and then get to work to improve every single one of them. And do it for every other area of your business, from finance to operations.

This isn't rocket science, but it IS a science, and Marginal Gains is arguably THE most powerful strategy at your disposal.

Let's put this into practice, shall we?

I'm going to take one element of your Lead Generation System to show you how you can do this.

Let's say you use an automated webinar as your Crowd Puller.

Now, when it comes to maximising the results of your webinar, it's not just about the webinar itself but also what comes before and after it.

For example, there are six individual steps you can look to improve and optimise when it comes to your webinar, and each element has multiple Marginal Gains which can be taken advantage of.

It's important you DON'T focus just on your actual webinar. In fact, imagine your webinar is like an iceberg, as shown in Figure 12.4.

Ninety percent of it is under water.

Your webinar itself is the tip of the iceberg, and the other five steps are below the water.

Your Perfect Clients ... the ad that you're running, whether that's online or offline ... the webinar registration page, your Pre-Webinar Follow-Up campaign and your Post-Webinar Follow-Up campaign all contribute hugely to the success of your webinar.

The more improvement you can make regarding the Marginal Gains of those six key steps, the bigger the impact they'll have regarding the success of your webinar.

And the three steps where you can make the biggest improvements are at the front of your system ... your Perfect Clients, then your ad and then your landing page.

Figure 12.4: The Six Steps of a Webinar

Think about it ...

If you have a webinar that converts 20% of attendees into clients or meetings, and you improve that conversion to 30% so an overall improvement of 50%, that's great, but if you're getting only 30 people to attend, then that impressive 50% improvement in conversion will only result in an three extra clients.

But if you tweaked your Perfect Clients, your ad and your webinar registration page, and those Marginal Gains produced 90 visitors instead of 30 for the same cost, and you improved your webinar conversion only from 20% to 25%, the increase in clients is a staggering 15.

So, although I am, of course, saying you must focus on all six elements, my advice is to work especially hard at the front end of your system, because the Marginal Gains will produce magnified results across it. Hopefully, that makes sense.

So let's start with the element right at the front of your funnel, and that's your Perfect Clients ...

In Chapter 3 I took you through the importance of focusing on your Perfect Clients, and I want to look at that more practically now, when it comes to your campaigns.

So, what can you do in terms of your Perfect Clients to maximise results?

To do this so it's easy for you to understand, I'm going to show you examples of how we run our campaigns and how I advise you to run them too, so you can see just how important your Perfect Clients are and the effect Marginal Gains can have.

First, if you think of your Perfect Clients as segments and then layers, it will make it easier for you to see how you can make huge improvements.

For example, when we're targeting people to become Business Growth Mentors, we have three primary segments.

We know through our testing and just through the products and services that we provide that these three segments of the market are really, really good for us.

We focus on business coaches, executive coaches and management consultants. They're all profitable for us. We initially just focused on business coaches and then tested other segments and found that these other two were great, too. If we hadn't tested other market segments, we'd never have found these other two.

Now, what you mustn't do is think to yourself, okay, we know that business coaches, executive coaches and management consultants are probably going to be really good for our business, so let's put them all in one basket as it were, and then target them all together with our Media Channels and tactics.

The reason why that's not a good idea is you just don't know how well each of those three different segments are going to perform. For example, let's just say that we hadn't tested, and we didn't know that business coaches, executive coaches and management consultants are all very profitable for us.

Let's say we're starting from scratch, and we're just thinking, okay, they seem all likely to be really good for our business based on the analysis that we've carried out (Client Segmentation Matrix).

And then let's just say we targeted all of them together. The problem we've then got is that we just don't know which segments are actually working.

If you get decent results from that campaign, or if you get poor results, you don't know which segments of the market are working best or not working. So, strategically, make sure you define each segment and treat them each differently. Do not put them together with other market segments.

And then speak to them in the language that resonates with them. You could argue business coaches, executive coaches and management consultants speak the same language, but when we're approaching them, we're not going to approach business coaches and talk about management consulting. It just doesn't make sense. But if we're targeting business coaches, we're going to talk a lot about business coaching and how we can help them grow their coaching businesses.

To all intents and purposes, the campaigns across the three different market segments are very similar. It's just personalising and tweaking the 20% that you need to do to make the difference, and 80% are going to be virtually the same. It's just defining those individual market segments. And then, as long as you target those segments individually, you will know exactly which sectors work for you and which don't.

Let's take another example ...

Let's say you're targeting gym instructors, dieticians, performance coaches and conditioning coaches for your particular service. It would be a mistake to target them all together. You have four different market segments, so you must therefore focus on each one individually. This level of fine tuning of your market segments will make a huge difference to you and the results you can produce, especially through Marginal Gains.

Okay, so you've now got your Perfect Client segments sorted, and you're testing them.

But you're not finished yet ...

What you then need to do is start layering each of those market segments with the demographics and psychographics you identified when you created your Perfect Client Avatar Profile. As I mentioned earlier, it doesn't matter whether you're targeting business-to-business or business-to-consumer, each will have a number of different characteristics that will help you determine how good that particular market segment is for you.

If you're targeting businesses, for example, you've got the size of the business, industry type, number of employees, title or position of the person you're targeting and location. Then, in terms of the person you're targeting, whether that's business-to-business or business-to-consumer, you've got their gender, age, income, the car they drive, education, the type of dwelling they live in ... and so on. Then, you've got their interests ... what books they read, what other types of products and services they buy, what groups they belong to, what other experts they interested in ... and so on.

The way to look at all these different demographics and psychographics is like layers across your market segments.

The reason why layering is so important is that it allows you to break down each individual market segment into smaller, more defined subsegments, which then makes it even easier for you to see what's working and what isn't.

Hopefully, that's starting to make sense.

You've got your market segments, and then you layer the demographics and psychographics through them to enable you to pinpoint with laser-beam accuracy the segments and subsegments that are highly profitable for you.

The Venn diagram in Figure 12.5 shows how this looks ...

This is an example showing what you can do with LinkedIn advertising in terms of defining the market segments and then the layers, and then running campaigns based on your selections.

You've got two diagrams, each consisting of three circles. Imagine that each diagram is a campaign. Each campaign is targeting the same segment: Business Coaches. And each campaign has two layers, one based on company size, the other on gender.

Both are targeting business coaches who don't have employees. That's what 'Myself' means in LinkedIn. However, the campaign on the left is targeting females, whereas the campaign on the right is targeting males.

So, in other words, we're testing to see if gender has a bearing on results.

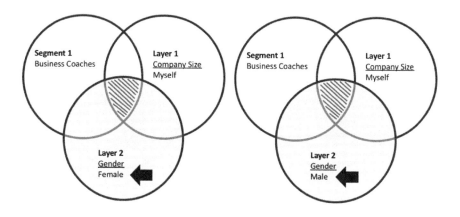

Figure 12.5: Using Layering for Marginal Gains

The great thing about most of the online ad platforms these days – and you can do this with Facebook, Google, LinkedIn, and pretty much all the others – is that you're able to specify the gender you're targeting.

Now, obviously I'm not discriminating between male and female; I'm simply creating two campaigns, one targeting males and the other targeting females, to see if it makes any difference to results (Marginal Gains), and often it does.

Hopefully, that makes sense.

The key is to set up your campaigns so that you test only one variable or one layer at a time, just like I'm explaining here.

For example, I could set up another two campaigns as shown in Figure 12.6 ...

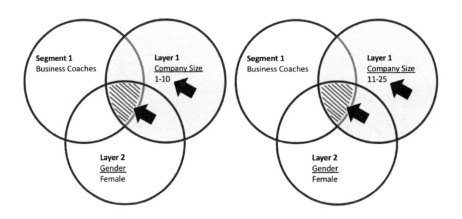

Figure 12.6: Using Layering for Marginal Gains

The segment is still the same, so we're targeting business coaches ... and the gender is now also the same. As you can see, both campaigns are targeting females, but I'm testing the company size layer.

One is targeting 1–10 employees, the other, 11–25.

I could also add a third and fourth campaign with those targeting 26–50 employees and 51–100 employees. Then I've got four campaigns testing four different employee sizes. This is easy to do AND is incredibly effective AND will deliver results quicker for you because of the effects of Marginal Gains.

Now, although I obviously know what works ... when you're starting out you really don't know, and even when you've done your research, looked at your own client base, and let's just say, for argument's sake, 60% of your clients are female and 40% are male ... you'll still want to target both genders.

But when you start advertising, it depends on the Media Channel (in terms of the numbers of females and males that use that specific channel) how successful a campaign is going to be, and other Media Channels will vary in terms of the results.

I would never pre-judge it, but let's say you run a business where 95% of clients are female, then even if both males and females are Perfect Clients, it makes complete sense to target females, because it's going to be more profitable to do that.

If it's a male-dominated client base, then, again, it makes sense just to target males, because the campaign will be more successful.

Generally speaking, if it's a mix, then I'd definitely test gender, and it's the same with all the other layers.

Now let's talk about the 'sweet spot'.

What you're looking for is that sweet spot right in the middle. You can see in Figure 12.6 that that's where all three circles intersect. I've used shading to show you it. That's where segment one, layer one and layer two combine to produce leads or clients for you. That's what you're looking for, and you'll know when a campaign comes together like this, because it produces leads or clients for you as a consequence of them combining perfectly together.

Now, it may be that this particular mix of segments and layers doesn't work for you. That happens sometimes. But with this approach using segments and layers, you're able to spot the poorly performing campaigns quickly, and either pause them or change the layering or the segment.

The great thing about the online advertising platforms nowadays (and it's been the same with offline data for decades) is that their data is just so accurate, and it's improving month by month. They all spend millions and millions on data.

This enables the advertisers such as us to pinpoint your Perfect Clients with laser-beam accuracy. And, as long as you're segmenting and layering the campaigns wisely to take full advantage of Marginal Gains, as I'm showing you here, you'll quickly find these very lucrative segments and layers, and you can then scale and grow the business really, really quickly.

Of course, segments and layers aren't just restricted to online Media Channels. You can also do this with both direct mail and published media. It's as sophisticated and has been for many, many years. It doesn't matter whether you're targeting people online or offline, as the data is usually very comprehensive.

As I said, this level of detail simplifies the whole process of campaign management. It's logical and will produce stunning results for you once you start applying Marginal Gains.

And, just to reiterate the point, you mustn't combine everything into one big pot, which many people do, because when you do, you just won't know what's working and what isn't. It's a sure-fire way to throw money down the drain!

Often, people do this because they just don't have the expertise that I'm sharing with you or, sometimes, because they're being lazy. The same applies to many agencies who don't really have a deep understanding of Perfect Clients and Marginal Gains.

However, without this structure, you're never going to get the results you could and should be getting.

I speak with a lot of business owners, and we often see that they're targeting one specific segment. For example, let's say it's printers. They don't differentiate between gender, they don't differentiate between size, they don't differentiate between the position of the person in the company and between the other layers that I've explained to you.

It's rare that a campaign of this kind, where you're putting everything together in one solitary campaign, will be successful, and, even if it is, there's so much wastage in terms of ad spend, because there will be only certain parts of the segment that are profitable. That's why Marginal Gains are so important, and you can apply Marginal Gains to your campaigns only when you use the layering approach.

Yes, it does take more time and effort to put a campaign together based on segments and layers. Instead of having one campaign for everybody, you might have 30 campaigns or even more on this basis. But all three Media Channels, particularly online channels, allow you to copy each campaign, so it's very quick to reproduce, and then you just change the layers depending on what you're looking to achieve.

Experts rarely give up this level of information in terms of how campaigns should be run, because in many respects these are the crown jewels, but I want to give you absolutely everything we use for our business and our clients' businesses to enable you to make significant improvements. So, I don't want to be vague when it comes to maximising your results.

In fact, the people who are making a lot of money from setting up campaigns such as this won't reveal this level of insight, because it's too powerful. I'm taking the time to do this for you, because your results are very important to me. I want you to get to grips with what really makes a campaign successful and segmenting your Perfect Clients, and layering is one of the most important lessons I can give you when it comes to Marginal Gains.

So, that's how to use Marginal Gains across your Perfect Clients. Hopefully, that makes a lot of sense to you. The most important thing about this approach is not to put each Perfect Client segment into one big basket.

Test every segment, along with the different layers, and then you're going to know exactly which segments and layers work best and which do not.

Armed with what's working and what isn't, you can quickly and easily scale your business. Overall, you're doing this to cut out all the fat, all the wastage, and all you're left with are the campaigns that make you money. Then, you keep applying Marginal Gains to make them even more successful!

Applying The Science Of Marginal Gains

Before we move on, let me just reiterate that getting your targeting spot on right at the front end of your Lead Generation System is going to resonate through the rest of your systems to produce huge differences in results and significant Marginal Gains.

The second way to apply Marginal Gains to improve and optimise your webinar is the ad. Obviously, you have now defined segments and, as I just explained, have different campaigns based on the different layers. Then, you're going to run ads in each campaign.

And you should always test two ads or more.

We test dozens and dozens of different ads, and I'm showing you two of them in Figure 12.7.

This will give you a really good overview of the difference that testing ads can make. So, as you can see here, one of the ads is paused, and the other is active ...

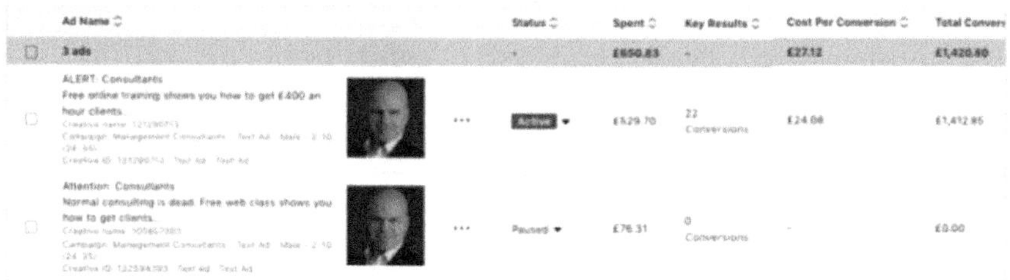

Figure 12.7: Testing Ads for Marginal Gains

In this time frame, which is the last 30 days, we've spent just over £530 on the top ad and £76 on the bottom ad. We've had

22 conversions on the top ad at a cost per conversion of just over £24 and zero conversions on the bottom ad. You can see that the ads are different: the main headline is different. One says, 'ALERT: Consultants'. The other says 'Attention: Consultants'. So, this is our management consultant segment. In an ideal world, I'd say 'alert, management consultants', but with LinkedIn we don't have enough character space to do that. And since this campaign is going to show my ads only to management consultants, it's still going to resonate with them, because they are consultants, of course.

And then you can see the top ad says, 'Free online training, shows you how to get £400-an-hour clients'. This campaign is obviously targeted at the UK. Ads that target North America, Australia and New Zealand say '$400 an hour'.

The bottom ad says 'Normal consulting is dead. Free Web class shows you how to get clients'.

Now, interestingly, the bottom ad actually performs well for certain segments and layers, just not in this specific campaign. Just because an ad doesn't perform well in one campaign doesn't mean it won't perform well in another. That's a really insightful thing that, and was surprising to me when I first discovered it.

In terms of strategy, we create the ads and let them run. Typically, we let them run to around £70 with LinkedIn and then assess the results.

You don't have to spend that much, of course. You'll get a good idea with a spend of around £50 per ad on LinkedIn, less on YouTube, Facebook and Google Ads.

The reason why you have to let them run like this is that you've got to give each ad time to make conversions and collect as much data as possible. If I had got a couple of conversions with the bottom ad and I had spent £76, my cost per lead would have been £38, and I'd probably have let it run for a bit more just in case the next couple of visitors converted, which have brought the cost per lead down to an acceptable figure of around £25 per lead (£25 per lead is relatively high in terms of cost per conversion).

LinkedIn cost per lead is generally higher than YouTube, Google Ads and Facebook, but the quality in LinkedIn is usually so much better, mainly because their targeting is precise, and the layering we add to each market segment as a result can be spot on.

With Google Ads, Facebook, YouTube, however, it's nowhere near as precise, not yet anyway.

You can see here that the top ad is working really well. We've spent £530, the cost per lead is £24.08 and we've generated just over £1400 in sales. The interesting thing about that is that virtually all of the £1400 is recurring monthly revenue. It doesn't show the recurring revenue, it just shows the initial purchase. There will also be a few book sales in there, which, of course, are one-offs, but probably £1200 of the £1400 is recurring every month.

So, that's a prolific campaign generating 'three for one' return on ad spend (ROAS). As you can see, it makes a huge difference to test your ads, and you never know what's going to work best until you run the test. Imagine if I had gone with only the bottom ad and not tested the top ad too. I'd have concluded the campaign was a flop and paused it. Once again this shows the magnitude of what Marginal Gains can do for you.

I've been in this game a long, long time, since the late nineties, yet I still test, because even though I can make calculated predictions, I can still be surprised by which ad performs better.

One thing to add here is that we do test a lot of different images, and you must, too. For example, for our campaigns, we test female and male pictures. If it's a male, we unfortunately use my ugly face, but if it's female, we use a stock photo like the one shown in Figure 12.8 ...

Figures 12.8 and 12.9: Female Images

We'd then crop it as shown in Figure 12.9, so it's ready to use. Again, it works sometimes with a female market, but not always.

And also, it sometimes works with a male market, and sometimes it doesn't. Again, we always test male and female images, because you just don't know which one's going to work better. We've also found, particularly with LinkedIn, that headshot photos work best, better than any other types of images. Okay, that hopefully shows you the huge value in testing your ads and the Marginal Gains you can achieve with them.

Remember, right at the start, I spoke about the impact of Marginal Gains of just 1%. The Marginal Gains in this example are off the chart, but you can achieve that only through testing.

Let's now move on to the third element that will make a huge difference in terms of maximising the results of your webinar ... and that's your webinar registration landing page.

Just remember, I'm using a webinar in these examples, but you'd adopt the same approach for your Special Report or book.

To test your landing pages, you can use something called 'split-testing' software. And certain Web page design applications, such as Clickfunnels, make it easy to split-test your campaigns, but I prefer to create two or more landing pages and then simply drive traffic from two identical ads ... where one ad goes to landing page one, the other ad to landing page two. I've found that gives you more accurate results.

In fact, we'll test three or four different ads, and then we'll test three or four different landing pages, and we'll do that at the same time, because it's quicker. You don't have to do it that way and, actually, I don't advise you do, especially to begin with (follow the Minimum Risk Formula). That's just the way that I prefer to do it, because I've been doing this a long time.

Figure 12.10 shows a good example.

These are two active ads. As you can see, they're exactly the same ads. The top ad is the ad I showed you earlier. It's a good-performing one, and it's converting just under £25 per lead, which is good for us.

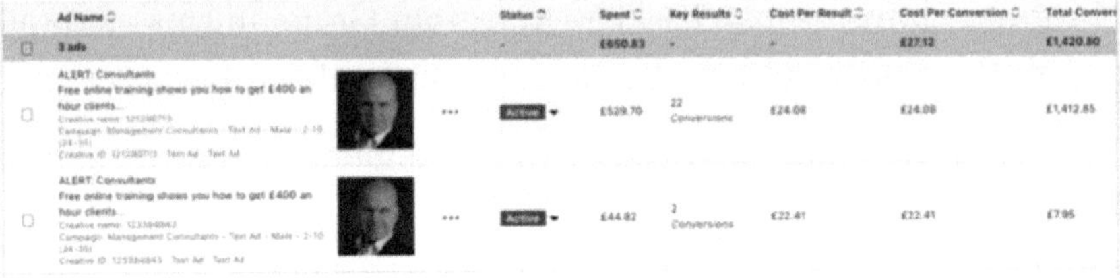

Figure 12.10: Testing Landing Pages

It keeps us profitable, as you can see from the sales value on the far right. Notice the bottom ad hasn't been running as long, because the spend is probably about 10% of the top ad, and it's generated two leads at £22 per lead. Actually, that's looking okay at the moment. But even though the ads are exactly the same, they're going to different landing pages.

We're not testing ads, because the ads are the same, we're testing landing pages ... and as I'm testing two different landing pages, that categorically means that the better-performing ad has the better-performing landing page for this particular campaign.

Hopefully, that makes sense. I've found over the years that this is the quickest, easiest and most accurate way to test your landing pages. Again, it takes a bit more time, but it's very easy to reproduce a campaign.

It's too early to say right now, but you never know, we might have found a landing page that works better than our current best-performing page. You can see the bottom ad has generated £7.95, but that's one single book sale, our *Business Mentoring Success* book.

Usually, that's a really good sign, because if people buy the book, there's a good chance they'll convert into a member. Figure 12.11 shows the two landing pages …

Figure 12.11: Testing Landing Pages for Marginal Gains

We're not testing the bottom landing page, because that's the 'control'; in other words, the best-performing one at the moment. We're testing the page on the top. The bottom ad shown in Figure 12.10 is running to the landing page on the top. And the top ad is running to the page on the bottom.

That's just proof of the pudding that we're doing this sort of stuff and doing it every single day, because what I'm telling you simply works and works really well.

That's the third element of improving the results of your webinar and applying Marginal Gains. But obviously you can see how transferable this is to all your other systems.

The key point here is that you must test different landing pages, because you WILL get big differences in conversions ... and again that means your Marginal Gains won't be marginal, they'll often be huge gains, just like the kind of gains you're likely to get with your Perfect Clients and ads.

I don't need to go through the other steps of the system, because I'm sure this all makes sense to you by now.

And remember, using Marginal Gains is completely transferable to every other part of THE MACHINE and the rest of your business. You have to be this analytical, this scientific. As you know by now ... 'Growing your established service business, isn't rocket science, but it IS a science!' and Marginal Gains is the epitome of that.

This is good. Think about it: if growing your service business was a creative thing, it would be really, really difficult to grow it purely on a creative basis and even harder for me to teach you how to do so.

But because it *is* scientific, you can take a more scientific approach to the growth of your service business, and when you analyse it, as I've shown you here, all you've got to do is take every step in THE MACHINE and then optimise it to take advantage of Marginal Gains.

And before I finish on Marginal Gains, let me just say that to begin with, I don't recommend you work through all your steps, one by one. What you should do is to look at the poor or the poorer performing elements first. Don't waste time on the areas that are working well right now. Look at the ones that are performing poorly, particularly at the start of your Lead Generation System such as your Perfect Client segments and layers, your ads and your registration page ... and then optimise them. Then, once you've done that, move on and start optimising the other, better-performing elements.

And, as you've seen, from just a few simple examples, the differences in results can be significant.

I'm not talking about tiny improvements either. I'm talking about 200% or 300% or more uplift in certain instances, but even if it were 1% or 2%, the difference over a combined 12 months and beyond would be huge due to the compounding effect of Marginal Gains and the results that they can bring to you.

Chapter Summary

- Using Marginal Gains is an easy way to scale your service business.

- Look at every part of THE MACHINE, take each step, and then apply Marginal Gains to it. Even a 1% improvement over 365 days is huge in terms of the results it will bring you.

- Don't limit Marginal Gains just to your MACHINE. Apply Marginal Gains across your entire service business.

CHAPTER 13

SYSTEMS, SYSTEMS, SYSTEMS

As you now know, a big part of THE MACHINE is systemising and then automating your Lead Generation, Conversion and Maximising Client Value. That's because systems work. When you systemise, you build certainty. You minimise errors, and, more importantly, systems help you to scale.

Everything so far in this book has been based on implementing THE MACHINE into your business, and although you'll be able to scale the growth of your service business, you must keep up with the operational side of the business. Otherwise, it will fall over, and you'll create a monster!

We obviously don't want that.

What you must do is also create systems for the other key areas of your business ...

- <u>Operations</u> (delivery of your service as close to perfection as you can get).

- <u>Financial Management</u> (real-time reporting on the numbers).

- <u>Human Resources</u> (employee recruitment, training and development).

As you already have an established service business, I'm taking it for granted that you've got these three crucial areas covered, to a point.

But when it comes to creating systems around them, I'd be surprised if you have documented step-by-step procedures for them, so that once again you can break each step down, optimise each one and ensure that when new people are brought into the team as part of your scaling-up process (see next chapter), they can get up to speed quickly and require minimal support and training (even though training should still be a big part of your employee development programme).

I call this entire process 'Systems and Procedures'. You are creating a step-by-step 'manual' of how the business operates in these key areas.

I can't tell you how liberating this is when you create systems and procedures across your entire business. But more importantly, it enables you to scale the business with minimal disruption. It enables you to keep up with the increased sales and new clients, customers or patients you're bringing into the business. And perhaps most important of all, Systems and Procedures can add massive value to the business on exit.

In my experience, very few service businesses have a detailed Systems and Procedures manual.

Of course, it takes time to produce, but it can be created over a few months. Better still, you can give ownership to each individual department in your business so they create it (not you).

This empowers your team, and, when done right, you'll create a culture of continual improvement across the business, so standards are increased and maintained.

Perfection is NOT attainable (you know that, right?), but striving for it will always deliver improved performance and results. And that's in reality what your Systems and Procedures are focused on. They minimise 'dropped balls'. They minimise mistakes. They get everyone working the same way. In short, they deliver improved results no matter how quickly you scale your business.

The hard part, of course, is where do you start?

Well, the good news is that I've developed a simple Framework that you can use that will give you the structure of your Systems and Procedures manual.

It doesn't matter what services you sell, this approach is universal in its application.

Let me take you through it ...

STEP #1: Create Your Vision, Mission and Core Values Charter

I could write a whole book on this topic and the virtues of creating what I call a 'VMC Charter'. As your team will all be working off your Systems and Procedures manual, putting your 'VMC Charter' at the front of it makes a lot of sense. They get reminded of it every time they open the S&P manual.

Ideally, your VMC Charter is a one-page document.

Your *vision* describes where the business aims to get to in the future.

The *mission* is how you will achieve the vision.

And the *core values* are the fundamental beliefs of yourself, the team and the business.

All three are very important.

They give you clarity on where you are today, where you want to get to and what you stand by to get there. More importantly, they get everyone in your business all pulling in the same direction.

To make this easier for you to picture what each element consists of, here's the VMC Charter I created for us and our community of Business Growth Mentors ...

The Vision is to revolutionise the marketplace by delivering world-class, results-driven and affordable business mentoring to the world's SME market.

The Mission is to significantly impact and transform the life and business of any SME business owner looking to grow, increase profits and build value, and do it cost-effectively with world-class Business Mentors.

And the Core Values are ...

1. Client obsessed.

2. Results first.

3. Our clients' success is our success.

4. Give the industry the respect it deserves.

5. Think BIG ... always.

6. Continual self-improvement (personal excellence).

7. Work hard and work smart.

8. Loyalty at all times.

9. World class isn't good enough. Constantly strive for better.

10. Perfect practice ... makes perfect.

11. The highest standards of professionalism always.

12. Lean and frugal.

13. Simplicity (less is more).

14. We never fail ... just learn.

15. Never, ever give up.

16. Your glass is always half full.

17. Take responsibility, always.

18. Integrity.

19. All in.

20. This is 'Day 1' of the Mentoring Revolution.

Until you create your own VMC Charter, you really won't appreciate how much difference it makes to your business. Just trust me when I say it will have a big impact throughout your organisation, and it extends through to your clients, customers or patients, too.

To help you create your own Charter, I've developed a 'VMC Charter Template' which you can access here ...

<u>www.the</u>machine.co.uk/book-resources

STEP #2: List all the high-level primary tasks in your business that need to get done

Next, you simply look at the three key areas of your business (operations, financial management and human resources) and for each area write down all the high-level primary tasks that need to get done.

For example, as I mentioned earlier, when we get a new client, one of the most important operational steps is that we run what we call a 'Systems Workshop'. This is usually held at a hotel, and we spend the whole day building out THE MACHINE specific to the client. So, the high-level task in this case would be the 'Systems Workshop'.

STEP #3: Break each task down into stages

Then, one-by-one, you simply go through each high-level task and break it down into stages.

So, for our Systems Workshop, for example, these are the stages ...

<u>Stage 1:</u> Arrange Date with Client.

<u>Stage 2:</u> Book Hotel.

<u>Stage 3:</u> Send Client System Workshop Confirmation Email.

<u>Stage 4:</u> Deliver the Systems Workshop.

<u>Stage 5:</u> Send Post-Workshop Summary Documents.

STEP #4: Break each stage down into precise steps (What does perfect 'look like'?)

Next, simply take each stage and break it down into steps. Some stages will require just one step, others a dozen or more.

For instance, in the example above, Stages 1, 2 and 3 have only one step each, whereas Stages 4 and 5 have multiple steps.

For example, the steps for the 'Delivery of the Systems Workshop' are as follows ...

Step 1: Meet and Greet Client.

Step 2: Introduction to the Day.

Step 3: Objectives.

Step 4: Build the Lead Generation System.

Step 5: Build the Conversion System.

Step 6: Build the Maximising Client Value System.

Step 7: Summary and Depart.

To give you an example of how all this looks, take a look at figures 13.1 and 13.2.

Figure 13.1 shows the front page of the Systems and Procedures manual.

Systems & Procedures

The Mentors NO Selling Prospect-To-Client Management System

MentorSuccess.com

Figure 13.1: The Front Page of the S&P Document for One of Our High-Level Operational Tasks

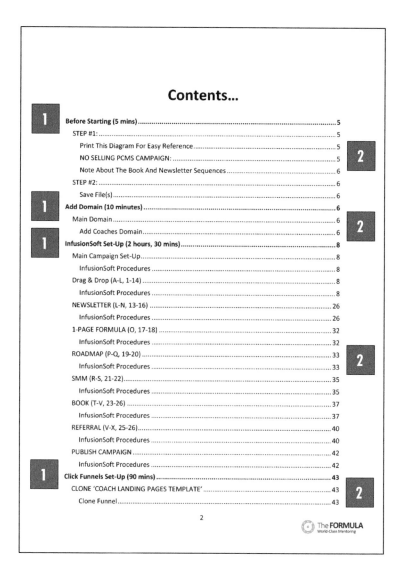

Contents...

1 Before Starting (5 mins) 5
    STEP #1: 5
        Print This Diagram For Easy Reference.. 5
        NO SELLING PCMS CAMPAIGN: 5 **2**
        Note About The Book And Newsletter Sequences 6
    STEP #2: 6
        Save File(s) 6
1 Add Domain (10 minutes) 6
        Main Domain 6
        Add Coaches Domain.. 6 **2**
1 InfusionSoft Set-Up (2 hours, 30 mins) 8
        Main Campaign Set-Up... 8
          InfusionSoft Procedures 8
        Drag & Drop (A-L, 1-14) 8
          InfusionSoft Procedures 8
        NEWSLETTER (L-N, 13-16) 26
          InfusionSoft Procedures 26
        1-PAGE FORMULA (O, 17-18) 32
          InfusionSoft Procedures 32
        ROADMAP (P-Q, 19-20) 33
          InfusionSoft Procedures 33 **2**
        SMM (R-S, 21-22).. 35
          InfusionSoft Procedures 35
        BOOK (T-V, 23-26) 37
          InfusionSoft Procedures 37
        REFERRAL (V-X, 25-26).. 40
          InfusionSoft Procedures 40
        PUBLISH CAMPAIGN 42
          InfusionSoft Procedures 42
1 Click Funnels Set-Up (90 mins) 43
        CLONE 'COACH LANDING PAGES TEMPLATE' 43
        Clone Funnel.. 43 **2**

2

The **FORMULA**
World-Class Mentoring

*Figure 13.2: The Table of Contents Showing (1) the Stages
and (2) the Steps for Each Stage*

Figure 13.2 shows a table of contents listing the high-level tasks, the stages and then the steps for a huge operational procedure in our business that focuses on setting up the online infrastructure for each of our Business Growth Mentors.

STEP #5: Explain how each step is completed (videos, documents, checklists, etc.)

Steps 2–4 create your Framework for building any system. I've used this approach for years, and it never breaks! Next, you need to 'put meat on the bone'. In other words, you need to describe and explain in precise detail how each of the steps are completed to the highest level of competence.

In the early days, we would simply have a document that would detail each of the steps. This is still a very effective way of explaining in finite detail what needs to be done for each step. But now we use video as well, which brings many of your steps to life, and makes it easier for people who are more visual and auditory.

Add templates and checklists where relevant, as well. Basically, you want to include everything needed to ensure anyone with the right level of expertise for that particular task can complete it *every time*, even the first time, to a very high level of proficiency and competency.

STEP #6: Automate (not everything can be automated, but EVERYTHING can be systemised!)

Then, look at each of the steps and see what (if any) can be automated so you take out the 'human factor'.

***

And that's how you systemise everything in your business so you can scale up INTERNALLY to match the growth of your business and do it with as little disruption as possible as more and more Perfect Clients are being brought into the business.

The ideal scenario is to get each team member responsible for the high-level tasks to create the S&P for that task so they take ownership of it. If you give them the process I've just taken you through, or better still, you create one of the task S&Ps first and show them how it should be, then they'll find it relatively easy to create.

The key, though, is to start building your S&P manual now so that when you do start to scale, your business internally can keep pace. It may seem like a huge burden in terms of time and effort, but I can assure you, it's what sets apart the world-class from the ordinary ... and it will make scaling so much easier and pain free.

Chapter Summary

• Systems allow you to scale and get things done by others with little or no experience to a high level of competency.

• The six-step process to build out your systems is simple:

Step 1: Create Your VMC Charter.
Step 2: List all the high-level primary tasks in your business that need to get done.
Step 3: Break each task down into stages.
Step 4: Break each stage down into precise steps.
Step 5: Explain how each step is completed.
Step 6: Automate.

CHAPTER 14

STAFFING THE EXPANSION

You're making great progress as you scale your service business. But what we haven't talked about yet is how you staff the expansion. Since the pandemic hit in 2020, it's been harder to find the right staff, and in the UK this has become a big problem. As you know, if you can't get the right team in place, with the right level of expertise to service the expansion, then things will grind to a halt.

So, what can you do, even if there's a shortage of people, to ensure you can still build a team of people who help the business thrive?

Plus, what can you do to shortcut the whole recruitment process, which can often be very time consuming, even if you're using a recruitment agency?

THE MACHINE

Over the years we've recruited hundreds of people into our businesses. We've done it ourselves, and we've used recruitment agencies, but either way, the process we previously used is the same that everyone has been using for decades ... and still do.

We took the view a few years ago that we needed to change how recruitment was done, because, frankly, how everyone does it today just isn't that effective. More importantly, our clients were growing so quickly that recruitment couldn't keep up, so we needed a far better solution than the conventional recruitment methods.

I'm going to suggest some radical things to you right now, but if you embrace them, you'll never have a problem again when it comes to recruiting people into your service business.

First, because there is a general shortage of good people in most countries, you need what I call a 'Hybrid Recruitment System'. It has three key recruitment strategies ...

Recruitment Strategy 1: The Short Game

A recruitment system to employ people right now with the right level of expertise.

Recruitment Strategy 2: The Long Game

A recruitment system to spot young talent and nurture them over time to be valuable team members.

Recruitment Strategy 3: Team Supplier

Outsource various roles or tasks (identified by your S&P manual) that a supplier can do for you, but even though they are suppliers, you treat them as part of your team.

If you view your recruitment from this day forward as a three-pronged attack and follow my *Recruitment System'*, then you'll rarely have staff shortages, and you'll be able to keep pace with the growth of the business.

You'll apply the following 'Recruitment System' to 'The Short Game' and 'The Long Game' strategies. Let me take you through it ...

STEP #1 – The Ad

Your ad must highlight how good a business you are and why people should work for you. Whether you like it or not, you have to sell your business to prospective employees.

The online ad should ask interested people to send their CVs by email and then tell them to write, in no longer than 75 words, why they want the job.

Asking people to tell you why they want the job in less than 75 words may seem innocent enough, but it's a very important question. You'll see why in Step 2.

Here's an example job ad we have used for our business ...

Overview

The Results Only Agency is an exciting international organisation helping business owners and entrepreneurs all over the world to build and grow their businesses.

'The FORMULA' and 'THE MACHINE' are arguably the most successful business-building systems of their kind, and are widely accepted as being THE sales and marketing systems for ambitious business owners looking to grow their firms. We offer our clients, members and subscribers unique, world-class products and services helping them to set themselves apart from their competitors and quickly increase their sales and profits.

Vision

Our vision is to be the world's leading advisory business for people running service businesses, and we are well on our way to achieving this goal. Tens of thousands of business owners all over the world use our books, training courses and membership programmes to achieve enviable growth and profitability. We are building a world-class business, and we'd like you to be part of it.

Who We Are Looking For?

We are looking for an ambitious, highly motivated and conscientious <position>. You'll be working alongside one of the world's leading marketing expert's, and you'll be joining a team that is often referred to by our clients, members and subscribers as 'world-class'. The business is growing at unprecedented levels as we expand rapidly into the US, Canada, Australia, New Zealand and all other English-speaking countries (we are already very well established in the UK). If you think you fit the bill, then this is an opportunity you will NOT want to miss out on!

Your Requirements

- Passionate about marketing
- Willing to learn
- Happy to put the time and effort in to develop your role and career
- Possess good IT skills

- A or B grade in English at GCSE level (as a minimum)
- Good interpersonal and communication skills
- Must be able to work to tight deadlines and manage time effectively
- Willing to roll your sleeves up and put in a good day's work – every day

Details of the Role

- Content identification and creation for our social media platforms, newsletters and emails
- Managing and overseeing our online and offline marketing campaigns
- Reporting to the board on the results of our monthly activity
- Editing monthly newsletters ready for printing
- Dealing with enquiries from clients and members
- Working alongside our social media and ad campaign team to brainstorm ideas
- Managing our YouTube channels

The Package

Here are the details of the Marketing Executive Role …

- Starting Salary: £X per annum (reviewed every six months)
- Bonus Scheme
- Private Medical Insurance
- Pension Scheme
- Monthly Health and Well-being Donation
- Hours: X per week
- Holidays: X days per year

THE MACHINE

Why You Should Apply?

As an organisation, we put a lot of faith in our team. We take time to recruit the right people, and we offer a very attractive package.

Training and development is a key part of what we do, and although we have a team-wide training programme, each member of the team has their own personal training and development plan.

A big part of what we do as directors is to help everyone advance their skills, their learning and their development.

What to Do Next ...

Send us your CV to teamrecruitment@theresultsonlyagency.com together with a note in less than 75 words on why you want the role.

STEP #2 – Filter the Responses

On receipt of each CV, sift through them looking only to make sure they have ...

1. Entered in the email why they want the job.

2. That it is less than 75 words in length.

If they haven't done either of the above, they are immediately rejected (STEP #3). Those that have complied move to the next stage (STEP #4).

This is why the task of getting them to tell you in less than 75 words is so important.

If people can't even do this simple task or do it as you requested, then they are not suitable. It's an easy and quick way to reduce the numbers of viable applicants!

STEP #3 – Email the Unsuccessful Candidates

All unsuccessful candidates at this stage get the 'Decline Email'. Here's an example ...

Subject: <First Name>, thank you for your application ...

Hi <First Name>,

Thank you for your interest in the <Job> role.

Unfortunately, you haven't made the shortlist for interview this time.

I appreciate this is disappointing news for you, but we have had a huge response to the role, and although I was impressed with your application, I feel others are more suited to the role.

Thanks again for applying for the role, and I wish you luck in your career advancement.

Kind regards,

<Name Of Person Responsible For Role>

STEP #4 – Email the Successful Applicants

All successful applicants then get the 'Success Email' directing them to the video (Step 5). Here's an example email ...

Subject: <First Name>, thank you for your application ...

Hi <First Name>,

Thank you for sending your CV to us regarding the <Job> role.

Congratulations! You have passed the first stage of our recruitment process, and you are now on the shortlist from which we will select three people to interview.

I am impressed with your CV, and your skill set looks like a great match for us and the <Job> role.

All you now need to do is click on the link below and watch the video. The video explains what you need to do next ...

>> [link to video page]

Thanks again <First Name>.

Kind regards,

<Name Of Person Responsible For Role>

P.S. Simply click on the link below to watch a personal message from Steve explaining what you need to do next ...

>> [link to video posted on EVS]

STEP #5 – The Recruitment Video:

This is a game-changer for you. The director responsible for the appointment should create what I call a 'Persuasion and Task Video'. It needs to be only 5–7 minutes long.

Then, once it's produced, you need to put it on a simple Web page that you will send successful applicants to (identified in Step 2).

This is an example template video script we have used and you can model ...

<u><Role></u>:

Recruitment Video Script

INTRO (the intro should be standard for each job no matter what the position or who is doing the video):

Hello, my name is Steve Hackney. I'm the CEO of the Results Only Agency. Congratulations! You've passed the first stage of the application process for the position of <Insert Position>. Please watch this video carefully, as I'm about to explain what you need to do as part of the application process. First, let me give you a brief overview of the company …

We are an international organisation primarily working with business owners and entrepreneurs in the UK, USA, Australia, Canada and New Zealand. We have a compact team of X people working remotely from home across the world.

We have three world-class services …

1. List service with short description
2. List service with short description
3. List service with short description

We are leaders in our field, and our vision is to be the world's leading advisory business for people running service businesses across the English-speaking world to grow their businesses faster than they could ever do on their own.

Now, let me explain why you would want to work for us …

As an organisation, we put a lot of faith in our team. We take time to recruit the right people, we pay well and on top of that everyone is eligible for our bonus scheme, as well as our private medical insurance and pension scheme.

Training and development is a key part of what we do, and although we have a team-wide training programme, each member of the team is given their own personal training and development plan.

A big part of what we do as directors is to help everyone advance their skills, their learning and their development.

We run a hard-working but relaxed, fun and happy ship, and we will help you grow as a person. In return, we expect from you three key attributes …

- First, you must have an excellent work ethic. We do not employ 9–5 people who clock watch. We expect you to work hard and be dedicated to your role.
- Second, you have an insatiable appetite for learning. We are one of the leading sales and marketing companies in the world, and the directors have a wealth of experience. There are few better places to learn world-class sales and marketing.
- And finally, even though you'll have many individual tasks as part of your role, you're a team player and respectful of everyone else in both your department and the company as a whole.

<u>YOUR ROLE:</u>

So, that's a quick summary of the company. Now let's discuss the role of <Role> …

The <Name> role is a key position. You'll primarily be working alongside myself but also with the other directors. Your responsibilities are varied, stimulating and interesting, and will focus on the following tasks ...

- Content identification and creation for our social media, newsletters and emails
- Managing and overseeing our online and offline marketing campaigns
- Reporting to the board on the results of our monthly activity
- Editing monthly newsletters ready for printing
- Dealing with enquiries from clients and members
- Working alongside our social media and ad campaign team to brainstorm ideas
- Managing our YouTube channels

So, if this position excites you, let me tell you what I'd like you to do for the next part of the application process. How well you do here will determine whether we select you for interview or not ...

THE TASKS:

1. First, in less than 60 seconds, I'd like you to tell me why you believe you would be perfect for this role. This needs to be a video. We're not looking for anything flashy or professional. A video on your iPhone or any other device is fine. It's the content we are looking for.
2. Second, email the video to us at <email address>.
3. And finally, in the email, write down five words you think that other people would use to describe you.

And that's it. I suggest you watch this video a couple more times, to make sure we are the sort of company you'd like to work for. Thanks for taking the time to watch this video, and I wish you luck in your application.

Notice that you have to keep selling *why* they should join your organisation. Also, the key again to this step is getting applicants to complete a set of tasks. Three always works well.

You'll see how to deal with the responses shortly.

STEP #6 – Filter the Responses

On receipt of each video and email, a team member simply needs to sift through them looking only to make sure ...

1. They have sent the video.

2. The video is less than 60 seconds in length.

3. They have added the five words others would use to describe themselves.

If they haven't done any one of the above tasks, they are immediately rejected (STEP #7). Those that have complied move to the next stage (STEP #8).

STEP #7 – Email the Unsuccessful candidates

All unsuccessful candidates at this stage get the 'Decline Email' (the same one as step #4 above).

STEP #8 – Successful Applications Sent to Director

All successful applicants then get forwarded to the director responsible for the appointment.

Staffing The Expansion

STEP #9 – Director Chooses Interview Shortlist

The director then decides who to interview. The good news is that with this system, the director has so far spent zero time on recruitment, and now they have a list comprising only people who have sent in a 75-word explanation of why they want the job, a 60-second video and five words to describe themselves. It's surprising how revealing this information is.

Of course, the video is the most informative. You get a real sense of the person (it's hard to fake it on camera). And they have to put in time to prepare the video.

You should choose 3–6 people at this stage (move to STAGE #10). Those rejected at this stage should get the 'Decline Email' (the same one as step #4 above).

STEP #10 – Email the Successful Ones for Interview

All applicants shortlisted for interview then get the 'Interview Email'. Here's an example …

Subject: <First Name>, congratulations, you've made the shortlist for interview …

Hi <First Name>,

Congratulations. I am delighted to inform you that you have been chosen (ahead of literally dozens of applicants) for an interview for the Marketing Executive position.

We are conducting interviews on <Date>. The interviews will take place with Steve and Peter at our offices in <Location>. Your time slot is 9.30 a.m.–10.30 a.m.

363

Please can you confirm either by email to me (<email address>) or by phone on <Number>.

In preparation, Steve has asked me if you can write down five questions you want to be asked in the interview that will show your best side. Please bring these along with you.

Thanks again <First Name>. We are looking forward to meeting you.

Kind regards

<Name>

STEP #11 – Interview

We all have our interview styles, but these three rules have stood me in good stead over the years …

1. Be prepared. Watch their video again. Read their description of why they want the role. Look at the five words that describe them. Read their CV.

2. If they are even one second late, end the interview within five minutes.

3. Always have ready at least half a dozen interesting questions.

STEP #12 – Call Successful Applicant

Call the successful candidate and give them the good news. Call the unsuccessful candidates and tell them it was a difficult decision.

STEP #13 – Staff Onboarding

Make sure you put in place a system for onboarding and training the new team member. You should have already created a system for this.

***

The approach I've just taken you through will transform your recruitment. As I said, you'll use it for both 'The Short Game' and 'The Long Game'.

To all applicants, it conveys a highly professional approach that sets you apart from all your competition. It significantly shortens the time needed to recruit a team member, and it leads to a much more successful approach to recruitment (you get good employees).

However, my advice is to also add suppliers to your team. This is especially important when there's a shortage of good people. There will never be a shortage of suppliers that you can pay to 'join your team'. It also makes a lot of sense in this day and age of strict employment law that's been built, no matter where you are in the world, to protect the employee, rather than the employer. You can get rid of a poorly performing supplier with one phone call. As you know, it's not that easy when it comes to a poorly performing employee, especially if they've been with you more than 12 months.

Plus, because this is in effect a supplier/client relationship, you're paying the supplier to fulfil a certain role, and they are duty bound to fulfil that obligation to a high standard to get paid. If they get sick or go on holiday, or have relationship problems, you don't have to deal with them like you do with a 'normal' member of staff.

You don't have to pay into their pension or provide private medical insurance and the like. In other words, suppliers come with no baggage, and as long as you choose them carefully, they'll be a great addition to your team.

But this is key ...

Even though they're not an employee, you should treat them as though they're part of your team. This is key and rarely done.

So, invite them to team meetings. Give them a Christmas bonus or present. Invite them to any team bonding evenings (if they're in the same country as you) ... and so on.

The more you make them feel like part of your team, the more they'll invest in your relationship, and the stronger it will become.

But where do you find them?

You have limitless possibilities here, but I'd start with Upwork (www.upwork.com). Our best 'Team Suppliers' come from Upwork. This is a great site that brings together suppliers and clients, and it makes it very easy to find the expertise and skill sets you're looking for.

Apply the same thoroughness as you normally would when choosing to work with someone. Use the job advert I showed you earlier, except remove the tasks. You don't need to see their CV, for example.

One great screening tip here is that you should always put your name (or the person responsible for recruiting the supplier) at the end of the job advert. Then, immediately delete anyone who replies without using your name. That's because some suppliers just see it as a numbers game and will reply with the exact same wording irrespective of the job, and won't start it with something like 'Hi Steve, thank you for posting your job ...'. That will get rid of 80%. Then I suggest you look very closely at the following key elements that are 100% controlled by Upwork (the suppliers can't influence or change them) ...

- **Job Success.** This is expressed as a percentage. Obviously the closer to 100%, the better. Anyone with less than 90% should be removed.

- **Earnings.** This is the level of fees the supplier has earned through Upwork itself. Use this is a guide. It will give you more confidence looking at someone who has earned thousands or tens of thousands rather than someone who has earned just a few hundred, but that doesn't mean that the supplier who has smaller earnings is any less competent.

- **Work History.** You'll see all the jobs they've done, what each one was worth, what rating they got from the client and comments from the client about working with that particular supplier. This is the area to focus on, and having read through each job and the comments given, you'll get a real sense of how good the supplier is and how they work.

- **Fees.** You'll get a wide-ranging level of fees across all applications, so remove those that are outside your budget, and do your due diligence, as above on everyone else. Just because someone is very cheap, it doesn't mean they aren't exceptionally good. There are a number of factors to consider here: their location, their age, their experience, and so on.

You then want to create a shortlist of 4–6 suppliers and then start a dialogue with them. Look at how responsive they are and what appetite they have for working with you. Get a feel for them. Set up an online meeting with them so you can speak with them face to face, and so on.

I promise, you'll be pleasantly surprised with the quality of people on Upwork, and you'll find the right people that suit you and your company. But if in the unlikely event you don't find the right supplier, then widen your search. Type into Google the skills you're looking for, and then you'll have a choice of many different suppliers.

Now, with a 'three-pronged' approach to recruitment of staff, you'll never be in a position where you can't keep up with your growth, and you'll build a great team around you.

Chapter Summary

- To ensure you match your growth with staffing levels, apply a 'three-pronged approach' to employee recruitment ...

    1. The Short Game.
    2. The Long Game.
    3. Team Suppliers.

- Put in place a robust 'Recruitment System' that sets you apart from the competition, minimises time and money spent on it and results in the right people being recruited.

- Don't shy away from using suppliers to build your team. Often, it's better to work with suppliers than employing someone.

- Make suppliers feel part of your team, and you'll forge long-lasting and very successful working relationships.

THE MACHINE

CHAPTER 15

THE PERFECT SCALING-UP MODEL

In this final scaling-up chapter I'm going to give you the Framework for a truly outstanding business model that will help you scale beyond your wildest expectations. It doesn't matter what services you sell or where in the world you're based, or how big or small your business is right now. What I'm about to reveal is game-changing and often life-changing, too.

The model I'm going to take you through wasn't even possible ten years ago. Well, it was but extremely hard to implement. But technology has made it possible without needing a team of techies to put it together for you.

The model doesn't change anything you're doing in your business right now; it simply capitalises on the services and the expertise you have.

Figure 15.1 shows you what the perfect scaling-up model looks like ...

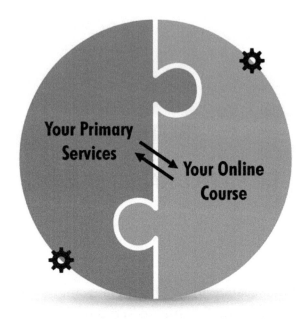

Figure 15.1: The Perfect Scaling-Up Model

As you can see, there are just two elements to the model. First, you have your 'Primary Services'. These are the services you're selling right now. I've already taken you through the four Scaling-Up Parameters you need to apply to grow that side of the business.

However, you can create a completely new dimension to your business simply based on your expertise and the skills of your team, and create an *online training course* that shows people how to apply YOUR system and your expertise to get results.

The reality is that a number of people can't afford your primary services but would alternatively like someone to show them how to get results themselves.

It doesn't matter what services you sell. You have developed a significant amount of expertise in your business in relation to those services, and that means you can extract that knowledge and convert it into an online training course.

But the best part about this model is that it delivers you an extra income and profit stream that is 100% scalable with EASE.

Yes, it does take time to build your course, but once it's done, it's done.

Think about this for a second ...

There are no limitations in terms of the number of people you train. Even if you have thousands of people accessing your online training, it takes no more time or effort on your part.

Plus, depending on your own ambitions, having your own online training course gives you the ability to reach international markets that your primary service may not be practical to reach.

And one huge 'hidden benefit' of creating your own online training course is that it improves your primary service, because it gets you thinking more about the best ways to implement the various elements of your expertise.

We created our first online training course back in 2009. Back then there wasn't any viable online training software or applications, so our developers built the infrastructure for us at considerable expense.

But the online training market is so huge now (worth billions every year) that there are some excellent solutions available for very little cost.

We currently have two flagship online training courses. One is 'The FORMULA', our marketing course for the owners of small businesses.

Thousands of business owners have been through the training.

Figure 15.2 shows the login page, and Figure 15.3 shows the dashboard.

This course was built by our developers through an application called 'Umbraco'.

We use this software because we have several purpose-built software programmes that we also make available to members, and Umbraco facilitates all of them (incidentally, I don't recommend you use Umbraco, it's not necessary for a normal online training course).

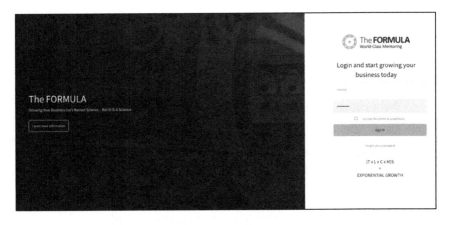

Figure 15.2: The Login Page for The FORMULA *Training Course*

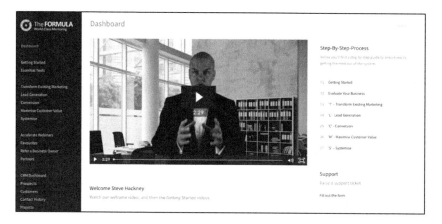

Figure 15.3: The Dashboard for The FORMULA *Training Course*

The second online training course we've developed is called Mentoring Success. This is our training that helps coaches, mentors and consultants create their own successful online mentoring business. Figure 15.4 shows the dashboard. This course is in an application called 'Thinkific'. It's one of the leading platforms to make it easy to host and sell your training course.

I have to say, it's an awesome application and was built to make it easy for people without tech expertise to have a fully functioning training course.

There are many other platforms like Thinkific, such as Kajabi, Teachable, and so on. All are inexpensive to use and provide the perfect structure for you to host your training.

Now, I could obviously write an entire book on how to set up, build and successfully promote your own online training course, so to keep things simple but still provide you with a Framework, let me take you through the high-level steps that will enable you to create your training quickly and how you should do it.

Figure 15.4: The Dashboard for the Mentoring Success *Training Course*

STEP #1: Create Your Course Sections

If you've followed my advice throughout this book, then creating your course structure is very simple. You already have two resources created that will give you the perfect Framework for your course.

You've got your productised service and your book. The high-level stages of your productised service should form the key sections of your training. The chapters of your book would also provide the key sections of your training.

For example, if you look at Figure 15.4, the left-hand side of the dashboard shows the high-level stages of Mentoring

Success. They're listed as modules, and there are six of them plus the introduction.

STEP #2: Create Your Lesson Outline

Next, take each stage in turn and outline as a list the lessons you need to create to deliver the result for that stage.

For example, Figure 15.5 shows the lessons under Module 2: Creating the Perfect MAP (Mentoring Attraction Package). As you can see, there are five lessons.

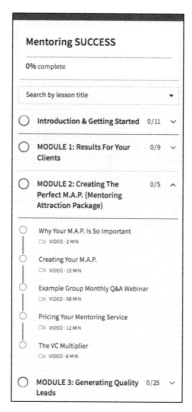

Figure 15.5. The Lessons

377

STEP #3: Create Your Lesson Videos

Obviously, this step is the most time-consuming one. The first thing you need to do is create the video for each lesson. At this point you have a couple of options ...

You can create presentation slides for each lesson and then record the audio over the top of them, using software such as Camtasia. This type of software enables you to record your screen, as well as audio, and includes a full editing suite so you can create perfect recordings.

Or you can stand in front of a camera and record each lesson. Using flip charts and wipe boards brings this approach to life.

We use both options.

But, for speed, my advice is to do as many lesson videos with you or a member of your team on camera as possible. You do obviously need an outline for each lesson, but not having to create presentation slides will save you a considerable amount of time (and money if you pay someone to do them for you).

STEP #4: Create Your Lesson Content

To make the implementation of your training as easy as possible for your students, you need to think carefully about the training content you need for each lesson (in addition to your training video).

Some lessons won't require anything more than a video, but if your lesson is specific to them implementing a tactic or strategy or completing a task, no matter how simple, my advice is to include templates and checklists.

Examples show 'best practice', making it easier for them to see what 'good' looks like. Templates help people to implement at a high level. Checklists ensure they don't miss out important elements of the lesson.

Plus, examples, templates and checklists add considerable value to your training when you're promoting it.

STEP #5: Upload Videos and Content

Once your videos and content are ready, you can upload them to the platform of your choice.

STEP #6: Promote

You're then ready to promote your course.

I appreciate that's a very quick overview of creating your online training course, but it will be a superb addition to your existing services and will help you scale far quicker than just scaling your primary services.

... and one last very important point to mention is that once your online training course is ready, it gives you the instant ability to up-sell and down-sell.

For example, those people who don't convert into a client of your primary services can then be offered your training course. And some of our best and most lucrative clients have come from people who originally invested in our online course only to then up-sell to our main offering.

This is why I call this approach the 'Perfect Scaling-Up Model'. You're adding a potentially huge additional income with high profits, and you have the mechanism to sell to more Perfect

Clients, because you now have an alternative 'service' to sell to them

It also reinforces your expertise and puts you in the top 1% of the top 1%! I urge you to seriously consider adding an online training course to your service offering.

Chapter Summary

- The Perfect Scaling-Up Model is to add an online training course to your existing primary services.

- It takes time to create, but your online course gives you a new and potentially very large and profitable income stream.

- Even if you have hundreds or thousands of people on the training, it takes very little extra staffing to support them.

CHAPTER 16

PUTTING IT ALL TOGETHER

Congratulations! You've completed a very prosperous journey. THE MACHINE is a truly unbreakable and unbeatable system for building and scaling any established service business ...

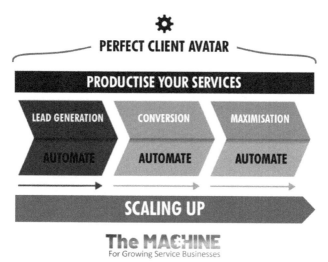

I've taken you through the importance of creating your Perfect Client Avatar.

I've explained how you make your services so much easier to sell and how to differentiate yourself from your competition by Productising Your Services.

Then, I've detailed how to put in place a step-by-step system for generating high-quality leads. I've shown you a system for converting as many of those leads into clients at the right fee, and a system for then maximising the value from all new and existing clients.

Then, I've explained how you can use inexpensive technology and applications to automate all the non-human elements of your systems.

And finally, I've taken you through the five Scaling-Up Parameters that will take your service business into orbit!

Yes, you now have everything you need to take your service business to the next level and beyond.

But ...

As you now appreciate, there's a lot to do, and most people simply don't have the time or the expertise to put THE MACHINE in place, because of their existing commitments running their business.

This means that if you DON'T take action, you will never get to position E on the Growth Curve ...

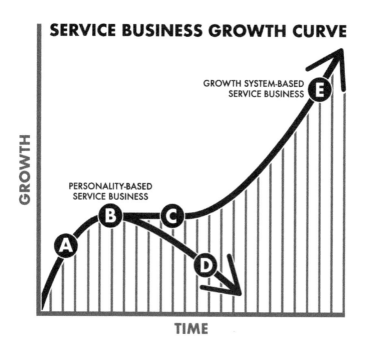

But I don't want you to just 'settle'! I don't want your business to stagnate between points A and C, or worse still start to descend to point D on the Growth Curve because you haven't burst the 'Personality Bubble'.

And as you're still reading this, I'm pretty sure you don't either.

So, why don't you take the easy path to point E and beyond and do it without lifting a finger? This next chapter explains how ...

THE MACHINE

CHAPTER 17

THE NEXT LEVEL AND BEYOND

If getting to point E on the Growth Curve is where you really want to be, and you're excited about getting there but don't want to have to 'go it alone', then you're going to love this …

Because you can have THE MACHINE created, implemented and managed for your service business … *without* lifting a finger!

That's exactly what we do for a hand-picked number of clients on our 'Done-For-You Programme', and I can do the same for you (if you qualify).

Our clients simply **outsource** the creation, implementation and ongoing management of THE MACHINE to me and my team.

And we can do the same for you too.

Let me and my team of Machine experts create, implement AND manage THE MACHINE on an ongoing basis for you. We even create, manage and optimise all your lead generation campaigns, whether online using the likes of Google, YouTube, LinkedIn and Facebook or offline with ads and direct mail.

To be clear we create everything.

We manage everything.

We optimise everything.

This is a 100% done-for-you service. All you have to do is meet with the qualified prospects THE MACHINE delivers so you can sell your services to them. But we'll even work with you to ensure your sales meetings are as powerful as they can be as part of THE MACHINE's conversion system.

We can get THE MACHINE built and launched usually inside two months, which will be faster, far easier and less expensive than if you did it on your own ... and even though you will of course be involved all the way, you only need to dedicate around an hour a week to the process, so you can get on with doing what you do best and that's running your business. Finally, you'll have a business building machine that will put your business firmly back on track and help you reach your ambitions and take your service business to the next level and beyond.

But like we advise all our clients, we don't work with everyone. So, let me tell you who the Done-For-You Programme is for ...

- It's for serious, very ambitious business owners and entrepreneurs.
- It's for people running already established service businesses.
- And it's for driven people who aren't prepared to settle and ...
- Those that are willing to invest in their business and other experts to get them to their intended destination far quicker than trying to get there on their own.

It's NOT for people who...

- Have small goals and ambitions. If you want to take your business from half a million to 700,000, for example, this isn't for you.
- Are terrified of investing in their business.
- Can't make a decision and procrastinate over everything.
- And it's not for people who think they know it all.

So if that includes you then I invite you to schedule a **free MACHINE Suitability Meeting** with Peter.

Peter is my long-term business partner and managing director and he will find out where you are right now on the service business growth curve. He'll ask what's not working for you right now and how we can fix that with THE MACHINE. And he'll explain exactly how we will implement THE MACHINE into your service business.

He'll also give you the opportunity to ask any questions and then if you both think this is for you, he'll arrange for you and your fellow partners or directors, if relevant, to meet with me personally to see if we can work together on the Done-For-You

387

Programme because I'll be frank, I have no desire or need to work with people who don't believe fully in the process and what we can do for them... or simply aren't excited with the prospect of working with us and what THE MACHINE can do for them and their businesses.

By the same token, we'll be spending a lot of time together, especially during the first couple of months prior to launch, so you'll want to make sure we're a good fit for you too.

This is a two-way thing of course. I promise you, if at any stage Peter or I don't think this is suitable for you, we'll let you know.

The Done-For-You Programme isn't a one size fits all approach and as I said earlier, we are looking for a specific profile of person and business so we can be 100% confident we can make a significant difference to your growth.

Then if we both agree we have the desire to move forward, I'll invite you to join the Done-For-You Programme.

However, because of the intensive nature of installing THE MACHINE into a client's business and the fact that I'm personally heavily involved, as I've just explained especially for those two months prior to launch, we only have the capacity to work with **3 new clients each month**, so make sure you book your Machine Suitability Meeting with Peter now.

You can get started now by going here:

www.themachine.co.uk/book-app

You'll first complete a short form. This form is important because it gives Peter information he can use to prepare fully for the meeting with you.

Then once you complete the form you'll be taken direct to Peter's online diary and you can book your MACHINE Suitability Meeting at a date and time that suits you.

Make sure you jump on this now if you want to have THE MACHINE working for you in less than two months, and then you're all set.

Just imagine what it will be like to finally burst the 'Personality Bubble' and take it to the next level and beyond.

You can absolutely do that with THE MACHINE in your business, along with me and my team to **do it all for you**.

So, go ahead and arrange your FREE 'Suitability Meeting' with Peter, and I'll hopefully meet you soon.

Finally, before I leave you, I just want to thank you for spending your time with me and for investing in this book. I know time is at a premium to all successful business owners and entrepreneurs, and I appreciate you putting time aside to read THE MACHINE.

To your success,

Steve Hackney

THE MACHINE

OTHER RESOURCES

Other Books Written By Steve

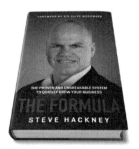

THE FORMULA – *The Proven And Unbreakable System To Quickly Grow Your Business.* Get your FREE copy here (just pay a small shipping and handling fee) …

https://www.freeformulabook.com

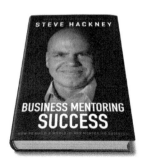

BUSINESS MENTORING SUCCESS – *How To Build A World-Class Mentoring Business.* Get your FREE copy here (just pay a small shipping and handling fee) …

https://www.businessmentoringsuccess.com

Say 'Hi' on Social

LinkedIn: https://www.linkedin.com/in/stevehackney
Facebook: https://www.facebook.com/SteveTHackney
Twitter: https://twitter.com/SteveTHackney
Instagram: http://instagram.com/stevethackney
Pinterest: https://www.pinterest.com/SteveTHackney